PRAISE FOR

Embrace Your Almost

"We all know what it feels like to have an expectation of what we hoped our life would look like, only to have it veer off onto a different path. In times like these, we need some help keeping our eyes up as we move forward. That's exactly what Jordan Lee Dooley does for us in *Embrace Your Almost*. If you are like me and need practical steps, hard-won wisdom, and a friend to help lead the way into a new season of promise, this redirection resource is what you need."

—Lysa TerKeurst, #1 *New York Times* bestselling author and president of Proverbs 31 Ministries

"Rather than reinforcing the pervasive shoot-for-the-moon rhetoric that our boss babe culture pushes, Jordan is a part of the resistance. Her book *Embrace Your Almost* tactically guides us on how to redefine success so that we can faithfully steward the good that God sends our way. This book heralds the message that this generation desperately needs."

—Amanda Pittman, founder of Confident Woman Co.

"Whether we've had the wind knocked out of us when a dream fails or we are finally breathing deeply after we release a dream that wasn't right, Jordan guides us with compassion and clarity to liking—or at least making peace with—our lives long before we reach the celebratory finish lines. *Embrace Your Almost* champions a life that is always under construction instead of one only satisfied at a completion that never truly comes. Jordan intimately invites us to join her in the space between disappointment and possibility, heartbreak and hope—whether in our home, motherhood, career, or faith. She reminds us that a life of almosts is one in which we're endlessly striving and never celebrating the fact that where we are today may in fact be beautiful enough, if only we see it through her lens."

—HILARY RUSHFORD COLLYER,
host of the *You're Welcome* podcast

"Jordan Lee Dooley is a perfect mix of wisdom and work-hard, and this book brings both. For when you don't understand and when you need a guide, *Embrace Your Almost* will walk with you, teach you, and lead you to the confident life you want."

—ANNIE F. DOWNS, *New York Times*
bestselling author of *That Sounds Fun*

"*Embrace Your Almost* is for anyone who finds themself in the awkward season of in-between. Jordan has gifted us with an insightful guide filled with biblical and practical steps that lend future clarity, even as they help us experience contentment when we are not yet quite there."

—LISA BEVERE, *New York Times* bestselling author

"I'm grateful for the way Jordan shares her honest journey and helps anyone who's had to wait or adjust their expectations in the season they're in to redefine success and contentment right where they are."

—RUTH CHOU SIMONS, *Wall Street Journal* bestselling author,
artist, and founder of gracelaced.com

Embrace
Your
Almost

Embrace Your Almost

Find Clarity and Contentment in the
In-Betweens, Not-Quites, and Unknowns

JORDAN LEE DOOLEY

WATERBROOK

Published in the United States by WaterBrook, an imprint of Random House, a division of Penguin Random House LLC.

WATERBROOK® and its deer colophon are registered trademarks of Penguin Random House LLC.

LIBRARY OF CONGRESS CATALOGING-IN-PUBLICATION DATA
Names: Dooley, Jordan Lee, author.
Title: Embrace your almost: find clarity and contentment in the in-betweens, not-quites, and unknowns / Jordan Lee Dooley.
Description: Colorado Springs: WaterBrook, 2022. |
Includes bibliographical references.
Identifiers: LCCN 2021030969 | ISBN 9780593193440 (hardcover) | ISBN 9780593193457 (ebook)
Subjects: LCSH: Christian life.
Classification: LCC BV4510.3 .D66 2022 | DDC 248.4—dc23
LC record available at https://lccn.loc.gov/2021030969

Printed in the United States of America on acid-free paper

waterbrookmultnomah.com

2 4 6 8 9 7 5 3 1

First Edition

SPECIAL SALES
Most WaterBrook books are available at special quantity discounts when purchased in bulk by corporations, organizations, and special-interest groups. Custom imprinting or excerpting can also be done to fit special needs. For information, please email specialmarketscms@penguinrandomhouse.com.

To Matt—
my teammate through every curveball
this life has brought and will inevitably bring.

Contents

Introduction

Even though I didn't like running, I joined the track team when I was in high school. Since several of my friends were on the team, I decided that I would sign up too. However, I secretly swore that I would quit if the coach made me run the four-hundred-meter dash. All-out sprinting for a full lap around the track? No, thank you.

But then, after the first few practices, the coach told me that I would indeed be competing in the dreaded four-hundred-meter dash in an upcoming meet. *You have got to be kidding me.* I considered backing out, but my competitive nature dared me to give it a shot.

The day of the track meet arrived. With my heart beating out of my chest and adrenaline pumping through my veins, I took my place at the starting line of the event. I heard the starting gun, and with six or seven competitors, I took off. As I rounded the last corner and entered the final hundred meters of the race, I was surprised to find myself neck and neck with an opponent, vying for first place.

Oh my gosh, I can actually win this!

As we approached the finish line, an image of Olympic runners on television popped into my brain. I remembered seeing them lean over the line to cross just milliseconds before their opponent. Despite having absolutely no experience with that tactic, I decided to try it.

And *that* was a terrible idea.

I leaned too early and too far, and instead of crossing the line, momentum carried me forward and I face-planted on the track, with my arms stretched out in front of me, fingertips just inches short of the finish. Everyone blew past me as I lay facedown in disbelief, with skinned elbows and knees.

The official leaned over and asked whether I still wanted to finish. I looked up to see all the other runners on the other side of the line, high-fiving teammates and grabbing sips of water. As humiliated as I was, I managed to bring myself to my feet and take a step over the line.

Just when I *almost* finished first, I ended up finishing dead last. I have seldom been as embarrassed as I was that day.

Almost

Have you ever found yourself in a situation like that? You know, where you're so close to accomplishing something great or reaching a milestone you've dreamed of, only to end up facedown on the ground, just short of where you expected or hoped to be?

I don't tell you this embarrassing story for the fun of it.

Trust me—I'd rather keep that tucked away in the archives of my bad memories and never speak of it again. However, I share it because I want to give you a picture of why I believe this book is necessary. Doesn't it seem that everywhere you look, there's another message telling you to go for the gold, achieve your goals, and take over the world? But what if your best efforts end in what feels like a face-plant, landing you *almost*—but just short of—where you hoped to be? Then what? Can you still be successful?

Look. I know that it's devastating—or at least incredibly frustrating—when you *almost* achieve a goal, *almost* reach a dream, or *almost* get to where you wanted to be, only to feel as though it all fell apart at the last minute. I know what it's like to think you've got the world at your feet one minute, then it's against you the next. I get how exhausting it is to hear cliché phrases about getting up and trying again when all you want to do is lie down and take a break.

Don't get me wrong. I'm a goal-oriented person . . . until I'm not. I tend to be a planner and a go-getter when I'm starting out on a new pursuit. I get a vision, and I swiftly take action to see it through. I chug along, chipping away at my plan day by day. If nothing interrupts me, I cross the finish line with a big dorky grin.

However, now and then something comes along and throws me off course just when I'm inches from the finish line of a professional goal or a personal aspiration. Whether it's an unexpected world event, a heartbreaking family crisis, or tripping over my own two feet, countless factors can come along and blow up my plan. Sometimes when that happens, I wonder if the goal I was pursuing was even the right goal for me in the first place, and it often forces me to rethink my pursuit entirely.

Why am I doing what I'm doing? Is this *really* what I want to fight for or work toward? If it is, how can I go about it in a different way? If it's not, what steps do I need to take to let it go or make a change?

Maybe you're a planner too. Or maybe you're not. You might be a fly-by-the-seat-of-your-pants kind of gal, and I can appreciate the beauty of a spontaneous spirit. Regardless of whether you're achievement oriented or more of a go-with-the-flow type, I'd be willing to bet that the life you have now might look a little different from the one you thought you'd have.

You may have thought that by now you'd be married with two kids and a dog, that you'd be at a certain level in your career, that you'd have the four-bedroom house, or that you'd be experiencing something else that just hasn't quite panned out (even if, at one point or another, you were so close you could taste it). Maybe you've faced one of these situations:

- That guy was *almost* Mr. Right . . . but then he changed his mind.
- That promotion was *almost* yours, until you unexpectedly lost a loved one and had to take time off, which caused the position to go to someone else.
- That marathon you were training for was *almost* a thing, until your kid got sick and you had to focus all your attention on caretaking instead of training.

Or maybe you're *almost* where you want to be but the finish line seems to keep moving.

And sometimes, when we *do* get what we want, we don't feel the satisfaction we thought we would. Perhaps the idea of "When I finally get XYZ, I'll be successful" is a half truth at best and a flat-out lie at worst.

Crazy at it sounds, I've learned that sometimes it's only during moments of heartbreak or disappointment that we have the "opportunity" to collect ourselves, consider all that we're doing, and clarify what we value and what success truly means to us.

Contrary to popular belief, maybe rethinking dreams isn't always a bad thing. That said, I'm not sure the answer to life's disappointments and devastating moments is as simple as "Just get up and try again." Instead, sometimes the answer is to redefine what success looks like for *you* in a world that's constantly telling you what you should do. This seems obvious, right? So, then, why is it so difficult?

Perhaps it's because the world can make us feel that we should want it all and do it all, all at the same time: *Crush it in your career. Also be a good wife. Have babies. Be a good mom. But, also, you do you. Don't let a family hold you back, and enjoy a fun single life. Drink a gallon of water every day. Volunteer for everything because you need to be a good person. Buy your dream house. Make good money. Oh, but not too much money because then you're selfish and greedy. Go on nice vacations. Don't forget to work out. Show up to that gathering so people keep inviting you. Stay in touch with old friends. Post on social media so everyone can see how happy you are. Have a morning routine. Help your neighbor. Call your mom. Do all the things.*

It's a lot. Some of the messages even seem to contradict

each other. No wonder it's hard to feel satisfied by anything we do! The moment we get married or start a family, we begin to hear about why we need to reach our career goals. Or the moment we reach a career goal, somebody starts talking about a biological clock and why we need to hurry up, find a partner, and make babies. How's a girl to keep up? On top of our own expectations and hopes, we face constant pressure to perform, meet others' expectations, keep up with timelines, and prove ourselves.

That said, this book isn't about crushing life, achieving every goal, taking over the world, or winning a race. These pages exist to help you define what success looks like for *you*, focus on the right goals for *you*, and run *your* race well—even when things don't work out how you planned.

It's about finding clarity and contentment—even in the middle of those almost-but-not-quite-achieved dreams—and making the most of the unknowns and in-betweens.

Why?

Because if we live only for the mountaintop moments—the huge, obvious wins—we'll miss out on the refining that happens in the valleys and on the journey. When we're hidden, when nobody sees our efforts, when we work for what seems like forever only to *almost* achieve our goal? That's the tension we'll spend a lot of our lives in.

Life—real life, where we have to make and carry out our plans amid unexpected challenges—requires that we are clear on what is a priority and what is not, so we can redefine success and move in the right direction (even after face-planting).

An Invitation

There's a question I want you to consider: Do you *like* your life? You may not love everything about it or be exactly where you wanted to be. But here in the middle, do you like the life you're curating each day? Do you feel connected with whatever it is you're doing?

I ask because I think sometimes when we find ourselves stuck between where we started and where we want to be, in those almost-but-not-quite seasons, we focus so much on the life we *want* to have that we fail to appreciate the one we *do* have. In fact, we may be tempted to dislike or even hate our one wild and wonderful life because it has let us down or broken our hearts in one way or another. It can seem nearly impossible to *love* our life when we're focused on what hasn't gone right. That's okay. I'm not asking you to love everything about your life. Life can be hard—and hard to love. However, I do believe we can at the very least *like* what we invest our time, talent, energy, and ambition in, even while we're in the middle—between where we started and where we hope to be.

I'm going to go out on a limb here and make an argument about something I've been learning in my own journey: sometimes unmet expectations and those devastating almost-but-not-quite moments are like unexpected (and often unwanted) invitations to reevaluate what we're doing, reconsider why we're doing it, and reorder our priorities so that we can steward the life we already have even before we get whatever it is that we want.

To be clear, liking your life doesn't mean you can't aim for more. It doesn't mean you can't hope, plan, or dream of possibilities. It doesn't mean you quit longing for whatever feels out of reach. It simply means you learn to sit with the tension of both disappointment and possibility. You allow yourself to simultaneously aim for what could be and make the most of what currently is. You know what you really value in a world that's constantly saying you should want it all. You redefine what success looks like for you, find contentment in what you do, and create a lovely existence, before you see the outcomes of your pursuits. You trade perfection for whimsy, delight, faith, and intention while tending to the life you've been given.

As I've learned to tend to life in the middle, I've discovered that our most devastating experiences and greatest disappointments can be either dead ends or defining moments. They can hold us back or they can clear away the distraction to help us see what matters most to us and how we will cultivate more of that.

When you allow your almosts (even the really painful ones) to clarify what you value and what success looks like for *you*, you might find that you can cultivate a life you truly like even before you get to where you want to be. You might find that you don't actually care about being the best on the track team or number one in your industry, you don't need to keep up with or outdo someone else to succeed, you don't want to break glass ceilings, or you don't need to have everything you're told you should want.

And those discoveries? The ones that show us what we truly care about, are called to, and can steward best? They free us up to *live* our lives instead of chasing more for the sake of more.

Clarity about your future and contentment in your present—even in the face of the pain or uncertainty that can come with almosts and unmet expectations—is ultimately what I want to help you discover in these pages.

If this resonates, pour a glass and let's hash this one out.

Embrace
Your
Almost

1

Redefine Success

I felt sick to my stomach, like I was going to puke. As I blinked hard at the results of a project displayed on the computer screen in front of me, my heart sank to my toes. I had invested tens of thousands of dollars into this venture, willing to take the risk because conservative predictions had indicated that I'd make it back three to four times over.

However, the actual data was showing that I might not even break even.

How is this happening? I wondered as I tried to make sense of it. *Did I miss something?* I had done my research, planned, and made calculated moves. Everything was set up for success, and I was so sure the investment would yield a generous reward.

I looked over everything again and again, only to come to the same conclusion: this was *not* going well. I felt so stupid! How could I have been so off in my predictions? *Why am I always so overly ambitious?*

Realizing how big of a flop this project could turn out to be, I called my husband and expressed how worried I was. He offered some encouragement and suggested we go out to our favorite little Italian restaurant later that night to discuss possible plans of action. Still in disbelief that we were having this conversation, I reluctantly agreed, and he made a reservation.

As he twirled his linguine onto his fork and I bit into my gluten-free risotto that evening, he said something I didn't expect. "J, I know this feels like a big loss, and your frustration with it is valid. But I also want to remind you that you didn't *have* to do this project. It was something you wanted to go for, but it's extra. It's not essential to doing what you're best at. And maybe this is a lesson in contentment in a season when you've been saying you want to slow down. Maybe it's an opportunity to focus on what *is* working instead of constantly trying to make something new work."

I swallowed hard as I processed what he'd just said.

He was right. Perhaps I'd let my ambition for more, more, and more run away with me . . . again. In an unexpected way, it was as if on that day, at a tiny table over pasta, he gave me permission to reconsider all that I was chasing after and whether I would allow what *was* working to be enough.

After we paid our tab, we headed home, changed into comfortable clothes, and read books under the bistro lights on our patio. The sound of crickets filled the cool evening air, and I took a deep breath as I thought, *Wow, even with this project not panning out, I really like my life right now.*

Sure, I had a lost investment to make up, but strangely

enough, I was reminded to be thankful for all that *was* going well. I paused, looked around, and breathed it all in, noticing that I felt gratitude on a deeper level than I had in a while. Perhaps that's because when disappointment or loss strikes, it reminds us just how good the very normal things of everyday life really are.

The Garden

A couple of days after our Italian dinner, I walked out my back door to see my husband preparing the garden boxes for planting, just as the sun was going down over the lake behind him. It was a late spring evening, and the golden light reflected off the water onto his athletic frame. I squinted as I walked toward him to offer a hand.

With my hands in the dirt, my mind jumped back to the previous August, the first time we had tried to start a garden, which I would later learn was well past planting season for most vegetables in the Midwest. The motivation to start one late in the season came after a hard summer for our family. I needed a hobby. Plus, I knew fresh, homegrown organic produce was so much healthier than days- or weeks-old store-bought food, so I decided to give gardening a try. Never mind that I'd never been able to keep even a simple houseplant alive for more than a week. (My poor succulents, one of the lowest-maintenance plants a person can own, always withered away because I was constantly on the go.)

But I felt empowered and determined to make that late-summer garden work. Dreaming about the bushels of spinach, kale, and carrots I was going to harvest, I looked through cookbooks to find delicious new recipes to try with my eventual vegetables. And for added luck—or at least to complete the farming look—I wore my overalls on planting day.

Week after week, I faithfully watered and weeded my first little garden. I eagerly anticipated those little sprouts breaking through the ground. I even found myself pausing in the produce section at my grocery store, certain that I was going to harvest better produce than what I saw.

Except that's not exactly what happened. That first year, despite my hard work, my garden bounty amounted to four measly kale leaves. No, not four plants. *Leaves.* As in, one plant survived, and I got a few leaves from it. The rest of my crop was either eaten by grubs or killed by an early frost. I could barely even make a salad with my "harvest."

As I picked the four leaves off the plant, I looked at the ground where my carrots were supposed to have grown but sadly had barely even sprouted. Clearly I'd failed miserably.

Or had I?

If we're evaluating success by the physical harvest, then, yes, I failed. However, if we're talking about my own growth as I learned about timing, slowing down, sowing, and tending consistently, then my efforts could be deemed a massive success.

Maybe those few kale leaves didn't represent a failure. Maybe they illustrated what's possible. Instead of viewing the one plant that survived as a disappointment, I began to look at it as proof that I *could* grow something. With a few changes, such as planting earlier in the season and developing a better strategy for fending off hungry rabbits and grubs, I knew I could get a better outcome. That one kale plant showed me that I can experience disappointment and see possibility simultaneously.

As my husband and I worked to plant our garden the following spring—ironically the same week my work project flopped and I felt like a total failure—reflecting on my first garden experience got me thinking about how we define success.

Many of us look at success as what we achieve: snagging a great job, getting a promotion, crushing a big launch, finding love and getting married, buying our dream house, and more. We achieve those things, and—voilà—we've succeeded, right?

That ideology suggests that if we don't reach our expectations, then we aren't successful at all. But what I discovered through my attempts at gardening—as well as through more significant pursuits that I'll discuss later—is that success actually goes deeper than attaining a specific outcome.

That's what I want us to consider as we walk together through the following pages—that we can be successful and create beautiful lives *even when* a specific goal or dream takes longer to achieve or doesn't work out exactly how we planned. We just have to look at success differently. We must dig below the surface to find what's most important and make sure that we grow more of it.

In other words, even if on the surface we seem to have failed, if we allow the experience to grow us into the women we were made to be, then we will have succeeded far beyond any superficial achievements.

We can experience great rewards even amid the hopes,

plans, and goals that *almost* work out but don't and even in the most difficult situations. In fact, I would argue that our most painful setbacks can set us up for the calling we were born to step into. That is, *if* we allow them to.

Please understand, I'm not trying to gloss over the very real grief and disappointment that accompany setbacks and letdowns. Trust me—I've had my fair share of the heartache that comes with them. But as you will see in the chapters to come, your biggest setbacks can become setups for success in the things that matter most to you. Success *is* possible—even if it looks different from what you initially envisioned.

Success Isn't One-Size-Fits-All

Before we can move forward in redefining how we view and pursue whatever we desire, we need to tackle our understanding of what success is in the first place.

What comes to mind when you consider what a successful woman looks like? Perhaps you see her with vision boards, bold lipstick, an impressive salary, and an air of confidence you'd give just about anything for. It seems like everything she touches turns to gold, and she blazes through every goal she sets for herself. Somehow she manages to do it all, apparently holding her relationships and revenue-generating goals in perfect balance, never failing to beat out any competition who steps into the arena—all while gulping down one Red Bull after another because, as we're often told, *success doesn't sleep.*

Or maybe you envision a successful woman as someone who has a white picket fence, beautiful children, and an adoring husband. She cooks five-course meals that would make Martha Stewart envious. Her home is always neat and tidy, and she has a garden that produces award-winning fruits and vegetables, which she cans and then adorns with beautiful hand-lettered labels.

Or you may have some other vision of success. But whatever form you imagine, it's accompanied with a lot of outward accolades, right?

And if you don't quite match the image of the life you desire, you might be tempted to think, *I'm not successful enough*.

Yet maybe success isn't when we have it all or look the part. Instead, real success is found in stewarding what matters most and ultimately becoming who we were made to be. When we understand and embrace *that* kind of success, we can make the most of each moment—and that is true whether we're on the peaks of great achievement or in the depths of disappointment.

Preparing a garden in the middle of what felt like a massive failure in my career helped me reframe the disappointment I was experiencing. In terms of dollars and cents, my work project wasn't exactly a smashing success. But in the way it dared me to be present, appreciate the small things, tend to the life right in front of me, and reconsider what I was really chasing? It changed my approach and transformed how I channeled my ambition. *That* was necessary growth. And that is part of what success needs to be.

Are You Ambitious?

Now that we've talked about success, let's look at how it relates to ambition.

When you hear the word *ambition*, what do you think? We could go with the official definition: "A strong desire to do or to achieve something, typically requiring determination and hard work."[1] But what does that mean exactly— especially as it relates to being successful women? I wonder whether you've noticed this: in some circles, ambition is considered a shameful thing for a woman to have too much of. Some view an ambitious woman as a highly competitive and determined female who steps over anybody who gets in her way. Others think of her as willing to take big risks, put herself out there, and even sacrifice her health or family to get the paycheck, promotion, or popularity she's after. After all, this seems to be what the girl boss movement, or hustle culture, that took over the internet for a while told us ambition looks like.

So, if we want to be successful, do we have to have *that kind* or *that level* of ambition—and if we don't have it, does that mean we have no shot at reaching our goals?

I don't think so. I don't think the type or amount of ambition a woman has should be the measure of her value or success, nor do I think ambition is something she should be ashamed of having. In fact, I believe ambition is a gift that God hardwired into our DNA. After all, it's ambition that gives us the resilience to get back up when we're knocked down and the determination to do something meaningful with our lives—whether that's in a business, career, or personal sense.

For example, that drive we have to finish a project, see a health goal through to completion, or make an impact on others in the work we do? That's ambition.

The truth is, we *all* have ambition. It just may look different for each of us. If you have a desire to care for others or make a difference in your corner of the universe, then you are a woman full of ambition. Can ambition get out of hand if left unchecked, causing us to overcommit, drive ourselves into burnout, or, as in my case, overspend in pursuit of more money or recognition? Of course. And some personality types are more susceptible to this than others (guilty).

Ambition is a good and necessary trait to possess. I would put money on the fact that you have a strong desire to do or achieve something meaningful, even if you couldn't care less about big paychecks, platforms, or promotions. I certainly do. I'm a driven woman with a list of big goals I want to accomplish in both my personal life and my professional life. One of my greatest dreams growing up was to have a family. It isn't something the world usually considers glamorous or sexy, but it's meaningful to me. Many of my other dreams pale in comparison, although there have been times I've lost sight of that as I overworked myself to reach career milestones. That said, at the end of the day, I have a drive to build my career, but I'm even more determined to tend to my marriage and eventual family.

Maybe having a family isn't one of your greatest ambitions. Maybe you want to be the first female governor of your state, have a thriving business, change the health-care system, or even become a professional Ukrainian folk dancer. Great!

Maybe you have big dreams to change the world, or maybe you have small-town dreams of a simple life. Perhaps you find yourself somewhere in the middle (hi, me too).

Regardless, ambition is that push you feel to pursue those important dreams and goals. At its core, ambition is really about *determination*. Determination is what we use to get up and try again after disappointment, to keep caring for a sick family member when hope grows dim, to heal a broken marriage, to stick with a journey to better health, and so much more.

Determination—ambition—is a good thing. But herein lies the problem: we live in a world that tells us we can have it all and even implies we should *want* to have it all. We should want to do more, have more, and be more. We're told to create vision boards and manifest, or will, our big dreams into existence—to work things out exactly how we'd like—as if real life makes it that simple.

Don't get me wrong. I'm all about having a vision to aim for. However, sometimes I wonder whether our ambition gets derailed. Maybe we've gotten used to gluing arbitrary goals and dreams to our vision boards just because someone else has a fancy beach house, a seemingly perfect body, or a million-dollar business and we think we'd like to also. Or, more likely, because we're unsure of what we truly want out of our lives. So, we write down goals or stick pictures of what sounds good onto our vision boards and then drum up determination to achieve those things—potentially setting ourselves up for discontentment in the process.

Even if they *are* the right goals, when we fail to achieve them, our disappointment can shake us to the core and make us question our direction. As a result, we may end up feeling lost, confused, discouraged, and utterly directionless.

When the world tells us that if we just check the right boxes and persist, we can have it all, it's disappointing—even defeating—when things don't turn out how we pictured. When our reality stubbornly refuses to match that expectation, what do we do with our ambition?

I've trudged through my fair share of disappointments as well as disrupted and delayed dreams, wondering how or whether I should go on. I've wondered how I can maintain my ambition—my determination to keep going—through frustrating disappointment, annoying discontentment, and even painful devastation. In the middle of those difficult yet refining experiences, however, I've uncovered an important truth: life is more like a garden to tend than a game to win. The more time I've spent working through this truth, the more I see how it's simultaneously simple and deeply complex.

So, let's go back to my first garden for a minute. At first, I looked at my gardening adventure as a game: I plant the seeds; I water them; they grow; I harvest and eat the vegetables—I win! After harvesting only four kale leaves that first fall, I wasn't sure I wanted to try again. But something within me—call it ambition—knew I couldn't quit on that note. It wasn't a game; it was a project that needed patience and attention.

Though planting a garden is a great endeavor, its failure obviously doesn't compare to seeing more significant dreams wither away. So, how do we move forward when we're stuck with failures and disappointments that perhaps we had no control over? We pause, fix our focus on what we're aiming for, remember why we're aiming for it, and either change directions if necessary or dig deep and find the courage to keep going—perhaps with a few adjustments in our approach the next time around.

As you'll soon learn, I know from experience just how frustrating it is to hit brick wall after brick wall, no matter what you do. I know how much it hurts to feel like your best efforts still land you in last place. I understand how hard it is to wait. And I know firsthand the sheer rage that bubbles up when something comes along and messes up all your hard work, perfectly laid plans, and should-be happily-ever-afters, making your life feel more like a story of happily-ever-almosts.

That's a thing.

I have also seen the growth that sprouts in the ruins. That kind of growth is often not fast, flashy, or fun. In fact, it's usually slow and almost always in secret, hidden from the world. It's the kind with roots that go deep—the kind that transforms ambitious women like you and me.

So, while I don't have all the answers about what to do when your hopes *almost* work out but don't or when your dreams are met with heart-wrenching disappointment, I do have a challenge for you. When you're faced with an almost-but-not-quite moment, dare to ask yourself these three questions:

1. **What do I truly want?** In other words, what does success truly look like for you? What do you value in a world that says you should want it all?

2. **Why do I want it?** In other words, why are you pursuing it? This is what I consider the single most important question because it will ground you and help you stay focused on what matters most so that you can pursue the right goals for *you*. This is so much better than striving to do something just because you saw someone else do it or because you feel like you have something to prove.

3. **How am I going to steward it?** In other words, how will you cultivate the life right in front of you—even if a certain milestone, goal, or outcome seems out of reach?

These three questions are essential in the face of disappointment because those almost-but-not-quite moments are often the only time we slow down and reevaluate. Of course, you can put your head down, power through, and try to pretend the letdown isn't happening to you. Or you can bravely choose to step into the invitation to gain perspective and find that you are indeed capable of creating a life you like, even in the tension of the in-between. Know why? Because as I said before, life is more like a garden to tend than a game to win. And you can grow only where you are planted, not where you think you should be.

2

Letting Go of a Good Thing

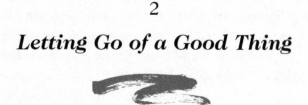

Have you ever had to decide to let go of a dream or some other good thing? I have, and I'd argue it's one of the more difficult decisions to make because it can seem so counterproductive, especially if it appears to be working. We ask ourselves, *Why mess with it?* even if deep down we know that what's working now might not be right for us long term. It may be a relationship, a career, or a commitment we've taken on that seems to work in the moment (*he keeps me company, it pays the bills,* etc.) but that doesn't fulfill us, challenge us, or serve a larger purpose in our lives (*he doesn't share my values, the job drains me,* etc.).

You may find yourself in a place where you have a difficult decision to make: Will you hold on to what is comfortable or familiar, even if you know it's not right for you? Or will you let it go, even if doing so makes you feel as if you let yourself or others down? This is a weird yet often inevitable "almost" we face—it's not one that comes out of left field and knocks us down but instead one that compels us to make a conscious decision. I'll tell you the story of a dream I had to let go and how doing so became a defining moment for me. Even though it was difficult, it created space for God to show me the next right thing to do.

A Budding Entrepreneur

Rewind back to my senior year in college, when I had taken up hand-lettering and began selling a few homemade decorative signs to friends and family. I knew I wanted to inspire people to display words rich with meaning in their homes, at their weddings, and in their work spaces. It seemed that I was born with an appreciation for a good story—for encouraging, meaningful words written creatively and beautifully. I'd loved to write short stories as a little girl as well as encouraging notes to friends before big events in their lives. And when I met Matt, my now-husband who then played on our college football team, I would write him "pump-up notes," as we called them, to encourage him before big games. I'd write motivational messages, like the famous speech by the hockey coach in the movie *Miracle,* or doodle Bible verses in different fonts and colors. Every design was different. Sometimes I'd draw Matt's number in the middle of the page, and other times I'd make a collage with photos from past games.

After seeing how people responded to my handmade designs, Matt suggested I try opening an Etsy shop. Quite honestly, I needed a creative outlet, and I wasn't too excited about the health-care job opportunities awaiting me after graduation. (In case you're unfamiliar with Etsy shops or a health-care management and policy degree, they couldn't be more opposite. It's not exactly a "tomayto-tomahto" situation.) Plus, I knew I wanted to have flexibility down the road, so I thought that starting something small would help make that possible. Thus began my first little business, an Etsy shop called SoulScripts.

When I opened up shop—from a storage closet in my sorority house (really!)—I had no formal training in retail or small business of any kind. I grew up in a home with entrepreneurial parents, so I certainly picked up a thing or two or ten during childhood. However, that was the extent of my business education, which didn't seem like enough at the time—especially since I was finishing my degree in health-care management and policy, not entrepreneurship. My classes didn't exactly teach me much about product development, customer service, or shipping fees.

During my senior year, I practically had to use toothpicks to keep my eyes open as I finished my homework on something I found incredibly boring, like health insurance laws. As soon as I was done, I'd bolt upstairs to the third-floor storage closet to work on my handmade art all evening and late into the night. While most of my friends were spending their Thursday nights out at the bar or a nearby fraternity, I came alive as I researched every little thing I needed to know about e-commerce, designed new products, packaged orders, and answered customer-service emails.

The year after graduation, the Etsy shop grew as I sold hand-lettered home and wedding decor, mugs, and more—

and my small-business dream came to life. Over the next several months, I began to share personal stories of overcoming negative body image, building a relationship, and navigating faith and friendships alongside photos of products on my shop's social media pages. Through SoulScripts, I was able to share my own imperfect stories as well as encouraging words that people would read, save, share, and even purchase to display in their homes, at events, or in their offices.

As I shared my stories alongside designs and product photos online, I received thousands upon thousands of messages from young women all over the world, sharing their own insecurities, hardships, and journeys to faith. After reading through message after message, I decided to write a social media post about the importance of community. In that post, I casually said, "Your brokenness is welcome here," essentially meaning, "You're not alone" or "I'm here for you."

I didn't think much of it until my email inbox exploded with hundreds of requests for products with that statement on them.

By this time, I was about a year out of college and had recently married Matt. Not only was I running a shop, but I had also started blogging regularly, had begun self-publishing devotionals, and was traveling to campuses across the nation to speak to college women about topics like relationships, body image, and more.

As the shop continued to grow and requests for products with that popular statement poured in, I shared what was happening with a dear friend of mine, Katie, who had become a mentor figure in my life. She was a big supporter of what I was doing and offered to help me manage my small business—and add an apparel line to my company!

We sat down to discuss how that would look and came up with a plan. I would focus on the pieces I did best: design, branding, marketing, and storytelling. She would focus on the aspects I didn't have the capacity for: sourcing and printing product, inventory management, fulfillment, and customer service.

We decided to try it and see what would happen. We started by creating two items to test: a crewneck and a graphic tee, both featuring *your brokenness is welcome here.*

A few weeks later, we launched them to the small online community I had at the time. To our surprise, they sold out in just a handful of hours. Katie and I were both blown away. Within a few weeks, we restocked and again sold out in hours. As I watched the orders roll in, I had to pick up my jaw off the floor.

What is happening?

The buzz on college campuses and on social media prompted us to upgrade from Etsy to a more robust e-commerce platform. That, together with demand for this "brokenness is welcome" message, catapulted us into unexpected fast growth. Our digital community grew. Requests for more variations of the product poured into our inboxes. It was bananas.

Because I was young and on a mission to make a difference, with bright eyes full of ambition and a bank account that needed funding, I said yes to just about everything.

You want me to come speak? Done.
Oh, you have a small budget? No problem—we'll figure it out.
You want a program about XYZ? On it.
You want ten colors of crewnecks? You got it.
It was simultaneously exhilarating and exhausting.

My dreams became so big and so exciting that I fell under the illusion that I could be Superwoman and pursue them all—all at the same time. Before I knew it, I was being pulled in so many directions that I lost sight of what actually mattered, what I needed to focus on, and what direction I *really* wanted to go.

I soon learned that true success and satisfaction in our lives comes not from saying yes to everything but instead from saying yes to the *right* things, no to the wrong things, and being okay with growing slow and steady.

Have you ever been there? When good things are happening, you grab at everything because, hey, why miss your opportunity? But if pursued with reckless abandon, our endeavors can get us into trouble quick. When we become so focused on succeeding, padding our bank accounts out of fear that we might not have enough, or seeking the approval of others, it can lead to overcommitment, overwhelm, and utter confusion. And those things are like weeds that choke the positive growth in the garden of our lives.

When you're overwhelmed, sometimes the wisest thing to do is pause, step back, and let some things go so that the right things can begin to grow.

Sometimes an "almost" includes *deciding* to let go of something—even of a good thing.

Making Difficult Decisions

Although many people liked how "Your brokenness is welcome here" *sounded,* they began to ask what it really meant or how they should explain it to others when asked.

Oddly, I wasn't sure exactly what to say. After all, I didn't intend for it to take off the way it did when I typed it in a simple social media caption.

Eager to provide an answer, however, I said something along the lines of "Well, this is like God's invitation to us to come as we are. We can reflect that invitation to the world." I found a verse to back it up and figured that was the best answer I could give. I mean, if it has a Bible verse in it, it's got to be good, right?

I felt like that answer was better—or perhaps sounded holier—than saying what it originally meant when I wrote it, which was "I'm here for you and with you in whatever you're going through."

To this day, I'm not sure why I felt the need to deviate from my original intent. I suppose I thought the initial meaning sounded lame. Or maybe just not spiritual enough.

Within just a few months, I noticed how often the message was misunderstood. I would see women share photos of themselves wearing the shirt, saying things like "This sweatshirt reminds me that it's okay to be a mess, because God loves me anyway!"

Each time, I cringed and thought, *Okay, yes, true, but also . . . that's not exactly the point.*

What was supposed to be an encouraging message of overcoming and hope was getting lost in translation. Instead, it seemed like many were viewing it as a ticket to just sit in their struggle. But I had envisioned it as something completely different—a reminder that, even in challenging seasons, we can find the strength and determination to keep going, especially if we lean into community and seek support.

Although it bothered me that people weren't taking away that message, the shop was exploding. The idea of stopping a moving train that had picked up so much momentum seemed ludicrous. So we kept going. We eventually added several other offerings—such as digital resources and community groups—on the website too.

Ironically, the more we did, the less peace I had. I noticed some drama bubbling up in our online groups, perhaps because, for many people, the message had come to mean "I can just be a mess, and it's fine! I'm welcome as I am!" In other words, some interpreted the welcoming and warm message to be an invitation to be rude to others or show up as the worst version of themselves. Whether it was leaving a snarky comment or putting another group member down, some people wanted their misbehavior or bitterness to be validated and approved.

Not okay.

Honestly, the whole thing began to drain me. After some time, I started to realize that I didn't even really *like* what I was building anymore.

About three years in, I found myself at age twenty-four, trying to manage a growing team, keep thousands of customers happy, create new products and programs, and build a brand that began to really lack clarity. As much as it might have been considered a success from the outside, the confusion and overwhelm I experienced behind the scenes made me question whether it was truly as successful as it appeared.

I mean, sure, people loved the products, and I'd learned how to connect with the right community through social media. But I was still unclear about the answers to basic questions: What is the purpose of this company beyond just inspiring people? What clear problem do we provide a solution to? What is this message supposed to mean? How do we ensure that it's being communicated as clearly and consistently as possible? Where am I taking this?

The confusion, as well as the overwhelming responsibility of it all, began to weigh on me, and the pressure to constantly outperform our results from the last month or year seemed to mount. These factors made it difficult to lead my team, to decide what to release next, and to know how to maintain the growth.

Have you ever experienced something like that? You know, those times when something you dreamed of actually begins to work but then takes over your life? Or when you're running on fumes but lacking any sort of direction? That was me.

I began to see that it's possible to *look* successful while feeling miserable without any clarity. If your internal experience doesn't match your external appearance, something is out of alignment somewhere. Until you get those two lined up, it won't matter how much money you make, how many people praise your work, or how awesome everything *looks*. You will always feel *almost*—but not quite—satisfied.

As time went on, I knew something needed to change. So I did the only thing I knew to do: I prayed.

I prayed for clarity, I prayed for direction, and I prayed for a step-by-step plan on how to improve what wasn't working for me. I prayed to get out of this almost-there season. I wanted these answers rolled out like a red carpet so that I could easily step right into exactly what I was supposed to be doing. Except that's not quite what happened.

I didn't get a mission statement or road map to sustainable success dropped into my lap. Instead, I sensed that I was supposed to step back from SoulScripts entirely. *What?*

Of course, that seemed silly. Why would I back away from something that was technically working—something that was popular and profitable? And if I did end it, would that mean my efforts had been wasted?

I mean, it was so close to being something amazing. If I could just figure out how to correct the misunderstandings around the message, slow down, and focus on the parts I really enjoyed, I *might* be able to push through. I didn't want to give up, knowing that it was *almost* where it needed to be. With just a few tweaks, it could get better, couldn't it? So I resisted the nudge for months and spent hours brainstorming how to course correct, clarify, and simplify.

The more I fought it, the more I felt that the answer was not to force it to work. I needed to close SoulScripts, at least for a season, to create space and find the clarity I was looking for when it came to my career. Everything had happened so fast that I hadn't had a chance to catch my breath. Perhaps by stepping away, I'd be able to do that. I wasn't sure whether that clarity and direction would include SoulScripts in the future. I just knew I needed to open my hands, release it, and trust that God had a plan.

About six months after that initial prayer, I finally told my small team that I felt we needed to close the doors to the shop and all that SoulScripts had evolved into and that I didn't know whether it'd be permanent or temporary. All I knew was that at the very least we couldn't consider reopening unless I became clear on the direction to take it and could steward it at a more sustainable pace.

Surprisingly, they understood and even supported me in the decision. So we made a plan, and a few months later, in August 2019, just over four years after opening the doors to a small Etsy shop, we held a weeklong warehouse sale and then closed the doors until further notice.

It was simultaneously one of the hardest and most freeing decisions I'd ever had to make.

I say "freeing" because as much as I hated to do it, it was like I could breathe for the first time in years. Oddly enough, I believe that the difficult decision and leaner season that followed ultimately led to more success than I could have ever imagined. Perhaps letting go of a dream or another good thing, though it may feel counterproductive, has the power to create space for something better down the road.

How to Let Go of a Dream

Tell me if this sounds like you: You need to let go of something, but you continue to hold on, even if only by a string. You wait for the perfect plan before taking a leap. You want certainty that you're making the right decision and that everything will work out once you do let go.

Maybe you're starting to sense that the new city you so looked forward to moving to isn't the right fit for you, or perhaps the degree you've spent years in school preparing for no longer feels like something you should continue. You know it may be time to try a new thing, but you keep pushing forward on the same path because you feel guilty for giving up on a dream. I get it—it's hard to let go of something, especially something that seems good. You don't want to give up on the thing you've invested your time, your heart, and your blood, sweat, and tears in. Letting go would feel like it was all for nothing. Even if it hasn't lived up to your hopes or it isn't healthy for you to continue doing, releasing it can feel like quitting. It can feel like you *almost* made it . . . but didn't quite.

Big decisions can be *hard*. Even if it's the best decision, that doesn't mean it's going to be easy. I'm finding that true, lasting success begins with letting go of what isn't right—at least not for now—even when it's hard.

You may find yourself in a situation like this now. If not, you'll likely find yourself faced with a decision like this at some point in the future. So I want to give you a few helpful steps to letting go of a dream so that, when necessary, you can release your grip and make room for God to do a new thing.

1:
Identify What Matters Most and Why

Don't just settle for what works; aim for what lasts. My friend Bob Goff said this to me recently when I had him as a guest on my podcast.[1] So, friend, I'm passing this lesson on to you.

This is simple yet so difficult for so many of us. It's difficult for me. Like I said, I didn't make the decision to let go of my first business overnight, especially because I didn't know whether I'd ever bring it back. I wrestled with it for a long time. And you may be in a similar place, trying to discern the right decision in the pursuit of what lasts.

However, when we're faced with the disappointment of a dream not living up to our expectations or the overwhelm that comes with trying to force something, the most important thing we can do is to step back and ask, "What matters most in this situation? What is most important to me? What do I truly value?"

In my case, when it came to SoulScripts, I answered, "Clarity and sustainability." While profit and popularity were good things, I knew they weren't what was *most* important to me. The most important thing was to have a clear mission that we could steward and sustain.

Your answer may be different. Let's say you're feeling unsettled about the guy you've been seriously dating for years. Even though you want to be married more than anything in the world, you may identify that what you value most in a relationship is a shared faith. A shared faith might be more important to you than companionship or a cute face. When you ask yourself why that matters most, your answer may be that your priority is faith in God as you raise your future family, and you know that you and your current partner aren't on the same page with that. That may be the sign that prompts you to consider letting go of a good thing.

Or if you're considering pivoting away from your current career path, you may decide that what matters most when it comes to your work is flexibility. Let's say the career that you've been working toward doesn't allow the flexibility that you've discovered you now value or need for your family. When you set out on this path five years ago, you didn't have a family, so that wasn't a priority then. Now it *is* a top priority, and it's become clear to you that this path is no longer the direction you wish to take.

Regardless of what this looks like for you, clarifying what matters most is vital for making a wise decision with confidence.

Dare to believe the truth that when you release something, you free up space for new things (and new dreams) to grow in you and in your life. The first step to letting go of any good thing is identifying the things that aren't aligned with what matters most to you. Always start there.

2:
Evaluate and Seek Counsel

Before making a rash decision when you're overwhelmed or emotional, consider who you can seek wisdom and input from. Whether you ask God for guidance, consult trusted mentors, hold a meeting with your inner circle (spouse, best friend, etc.), or all the above, take time to discuss the decision you're considering.

I've found it's helpful to set a bit of a limit on this, either on the amount of time to make the decision (for example, ninety days) or on the number of conversations I'll have before taking action (for example, no more than five or ten). This helps me avoid annoying the heck out of everyone in my life or stalling on a step I know I need to take.

For example, when I was trying to decide whether to step back from SoulScripts, I asked a few trusted mentors for their advice. In those conversations, I explained what was working, what wasn't working, and how I was feeling. Additionally, I was able to admit that I worried I was quitting instead of persevering and that I wasn't sure how to know whether it would be wise or foolish to let it go. After hearing all that was going on and where I was as both a leader and an individual, they were able to provide sound advice. This gave me the confidence that taking a step back wasn't a lazy decision but in fact was a healthy and necessary one.

3:
Make a Plan for the Open Space on Your Plate

One of the hardest parts of letting go of a dream is the unknown on the other side of the decision. We ask ourselves questions like: *What if breaking up ends up being a bad decision? What if I regret it or miss him? What will I do with the time that opens up when this person is no longer a focus in my life?*

The endless what-ifs can drive us into analysis paralysis. Of course, there's no way to predict the future or guarantee that we'll be completely happy with our decision. However, we can be intentional about making a plan so we have a road map to follow. This allows us to move forward and steward that decision with clarity and confidence.

For example, when I decided to let go of SoulScripts, there were a lot of things I didn't know: I didn't know whether my online community would be supportive or upset. I didn't know whether SoulScripts would be closed for one month, one year, ten years, or forever. I didn't know whether I'd miss it. All I knew was that I needed to let go of it if I ever hoped to see what God had in store for me.

With all the unknowns, the only thing that gave me peace (and the confidence to follow through!) was making an action plan for (1) how I would go about seeing the decision through and (2) how I would move forward afterward.

When it came to seeing the decision through, my small team and I decided we would close the shop with a warehouse sale. Then we decided on the dates for that sale (about three months in the future) and set a clear timeline with to-dos. We counted remaining inventory, gathered photos of the items, set discounts, planned an announcement for social media, and more.

Once that plan was set, I also took some time to clarify how I would steward the space in my calendar that would open once the shop closed. I planned to pour into other commitments on my plate, such as speaking engagements and writing the book I had started but struggled to finish because I had been too busy to give it my full attention.

When you consider letting go of a dream or another good thing, the empty space it leaves can feel intimidating and overwhelming. Although you may not have a new boyfriend, the ultimate perfect job, a new dream home, or the next opportunity lined up and waiting for you the moment you decide to release whatever it is you're planning to let go, try to think ahead about how you might steward the space that will open in your life.

Are there things you've always wanted to do but never had time for, like writing a book, training for a marathon, refurbishing furniture, or learning to play an instrument? Perhaps freeing up some space in your life will allow you margin to do those things. As you face the decision to let go of a dream or another good thing, also make a plan to do one of those things you've always wanted to do: take up piano lessons, join a running club, or go back to school. This way, you'll have something to look forward to when you step away from the draining job, the unhealthy relationship, the would-be dream house that has turned into a money pit, or whatever it is that you know you need to release.

It may not take away all the uneasy feelings you have about the unknown, but some peace of mind can come from knowing you have something to look forward to after you let go.

These are just a few key considerations when it comes to letting go of a dream or another good thing, especially when it seems as though you're almost where you wanted to be. I can't tell you that it's going to be easy. But if what you're currently doing doesn't align with what matters most to you, I can tell you that whatever decision you're facing, there is a way forward. And looking back, I can say with confidence that there *is* something beautiful—dare I say *even better?*—waiting on the other side, even if you can't see it yet.

3

Dream Again

I'm just going to say it: Those unknown voices of wisdom were right. Well, they were *mostly* right. They say that when you hold your baby for the first time, your whole world changes.

But I think it happens long before that moment. When you pee on a stick and it confirms that a little life is growing inside you, your whole world changes at *that* moment too. At least, that's how it happened for me.

It was a snowy morning in December 2019 when tears welled up in my eyes and I stood staring in disbelief at a positive pregnancy test.

"Are you serious?" I kept saying out loud as if someone were playing a trick on me, although I was in the bathroom alone. It felt so surreal! I took another test just to be sure. (I know I'm not the only one who's done that!) That one was positive too.

I decided I would find a special way to tell Matt and

quickly hid the box that the tests came in. This was our first baby, and I wanted to go all out!

I tried not to let on that anything was up, and the only thing out of the ordinary he noticed was my random decision to juice beets that morning. For the record, I'd never juiced beets in my life. I don't even like beets unless they're drenched in so much sauce or goat cheese that you can't tell they taste like dirt. But the second I found out my body was growing another human, I decided I'd grin and bear it because beets are healthy and, I reasoned, I needed to be healthy too.

When Matt walked into the kitchen and saw me juicing two big beets as if that were part of my normal Tuesday morning routine, he looked at me a little funny. "What are you doing?"

"Just making some beet juice!" I said confidently.

"Uh, okay," he responded with a perplexed look.

He walked into the other room to gather his things before heading out to work for the day, and I let out a sigh of relief, thankful he hadn't pushed the issue any further.

Just let a woman juice her beets, okay?

After finishing my juice, I went to Target on a mission to find something sweet to tell him with. Later that evening, I called him into the living room and told him I had an early Christmas gift for him as I handed him a box with a bow on top.

His face lit up as he opened the box and saw the positive test from that morning. "Are you serious?" he asked, mouth agape. I guess "Are you serious?" is the most appropriate response to a miracle like that. We spent the rest of the night celebrating, figuring out the due date, and dreaming up how we'd tell our families the big news.

When we went to bed that night, I curled up next to him and said, "Gosh, this just feels like the perfect year. With all that we've been able to accomplish in our careers and now finishing out the year with this news? I am just so, so thankful."

"Me too," he said, squeezing me tight. "I'm over the moon."

When Your Expectations Get Interrupted

A few weeks later, we enjoyed a big Christmas Eve lunch with my husband's family in Arizona. My father-in-law passed the rolls, and since we had just recently told them the big news, we talked about the baby and all that the upcoming year would bring.

Halfway through the meal, I got up to use the restroom and noticed light bleeding.

No, no, no! This can't be happening! I thought.

I knew the first trimester was often considered the riskiest time in a pregnancy, but I never once thought something would go wrong.

I looked again just to verify that my mind wasn't playing tricks on me. It wasn't. My stomach dropped, my heart sank, and a lump formed in my throat. Fear immediately set in, and I called for Matt.

A few seconds later, he knocked on the door. "Everything okay?"

I opened the door, tears welling up in my eyes, showed him what I saw, and told him that I wanted to go to the emergency room to get an ultrasound.

The ER was the *last* place I wanted to spend Christmas Eve, but since we were out of town visiting and I couldn't go to my local doctor, it was the only option in a pinch.

Matt told his family, I grabbed my things, and we left our half-finished meals on the table as we bolted out the door.

When we got to the hospital, they wrote down my information and got me into a room pretty quickly. I changed out of my sleek black jumpsuit and put on one of those hideous gowns—you know, the ones that make you feel like you're mooning everyone you walk by, no matter how well you tie it.

A few minutes later, a nurse came in, took my vitals, and asked a series of questions.

Shortly after she left, the doctor came in to introduce herself. Then she said that the ultrasound tech would be in to get me soon and that we would review the results of the ultrasound together.

Matt and I looked at each other, feeling the most helpless we'd felt in a long time. We're both go-getters, problem-solvers, and make-it-happeners. But *this*? This wasn't something we could work or dream or plan our way out of. It was what it was . . . and we both knew there was nothing we could do about whatever we were about to find out.

Before long, a man walked into the room. Not just any man. A grumpy, creepy-looking man. He introduced himself as Fred and told me he'd be doing an internal exam—a pelvic ultrasound—a pretty invasive procedure even under the most favorable circumstances.

Merry Christmas to me.

He wheeled me back, with Matt walking next to me, and began the scan. With my heart beating out of my chest, I reached for Matt's hand and squeezed it tight. Seconds later, Fred pointed to a flicker on the screen. "See that? That's the heartbeat."

The heartbeat? Oh, thank God!

I looked at the screen, laid my head back, loosened my grip on Matt's hand a bit, and breathed a sigh of relief. But that relief quickly turned to confusion. Trying to put the pieces together, I turned toward Matt and said, "Wait. So, then . . . what's going on?"

Before Matt could respond, Fred spoke up. "Well, you could still be miscarrying," he said. Just like that.

What the . . . Thanks for the peace of mind, Fred. I don't think it's within your job description—or very considerate—to share that kind of information so matter-of-factly with a terrified first-time mom (on Christmas nonetheless!).

We waited about thirty minutes after the ultrasound until the doctor came in to do a pelvic exam. Soon after, the nurse came in with the radiology reports. The doctor pulled her glasses from the top of her head and rested them on her nose before examining the papers.

"Oh, I see," she said, then explained the source of the bleeding—a small hematoma that can form during implantation. Then she went on to explain that this is common, and oftentimes these kind of things resolve themselves, but sometimes they do not. When they do, things progress as normal. When they don't, it causes a loss. Her only recommendation was to take it easy by going on light bed rest for a few weeks and hope that it healed. Then she suggested we pick up some pads too.

On the way back to our hotel, I called my mom to update her, and Matt pulled into a Walgreens parking lot. Since I was on a call, he didn't interrupt to ask what to get. He just went into the store and came back out five minutes later carrying a bag.

I didn't think much of the fact that I hadn't given him any instructions until we got back to the hotel and I opened the bag to see the kind of pads he purchased. They were the huge, diaper-like ones for *incontinence*.

Well, he tried.

It was late on Christmas Eve, and we were emotional, so I didn't want to send him out again. I put on my gigantic pad, pulled on my pajama pants, and went to bed with the shred of dignity I had left.

The following afternoon, I wiggled my way into some sweatpants so we could visit with family for a few hours. However, the second I walked in the door and saw them all enjoying themselves, I burst into tears. I couldn't help it.

Blame it on hormones or perhaps hormones and fear coupled together, but nothing felt good—and my expectations about this holiday had just been ripped out from under me. Instead of joyfully looking to the future and celebrating like I thought we would, I felt as though I were walking on pins and needles, struggling to remain optimistic in the face of such an uncertain diagnosis.

It's crazy how life can do that to you. One day can be the highest high, your whole family celebrating a dream coming true with you, and the next day can be the lowest low as you tiptoe on, knowing there's a strong chance you could lose that dream, hoping for the best but bracing for the worst.

I'm sure you've found yourself on that roller coaster in one situation or another. Just when it looks like a dream is about to come true, something comes out of the blue and knocks you down. Suddenly the thing you thought you'd have hangs in the balance, threatened by illness, economic tension, or another unexpected challenge. And in that moment, just when you need to muster up the courage to believe that things will work out, reality sinks in, the wait for an answer seems endless, and holding on to hope feels foolish.

With cautious optimism, we spent the following week praying endlessly, asking friends to pray, and fighting to believe that everything would be okay.

Everything Is *Not* Okay

The day after we returned from our trip, I had an ultrasound appointment with a local doctor.

"Do you think everything's going to be okay?" I asked Matt nervously as we waited in the lobby, as if he could see into the future and knew something I didn't.

"I do," he said confidently. "It's all going to be great."

I'm not sure whether he actually believed that or he was just trying to help me feel better, but I tried with all my might to believe him. A few minutes later, a nurse called us back and my heart began to race.

Matt stood beside me as the tech began the ultrasound, and I looked up at the ceiling tiles, silently begging God to make everything okay. Several moments passed, and she leaned in to look closer at the screen but still didn't say anything. Matt squinted to try to see any sign of life too.

Neither of them looked confident, and that's when I knew something was wrong.

Then the tech took a deep breath and said, "I'm sorry. I don't see a heartbeat."

My heart shattered as I squeezed Matt's hand and tried to suppress the scream I wanted to let out. We looked at each other, feeling both shocked and helpless as could be.

This can't be happening.

The doctor came in and explained my options, all of which were equally terrible, and then stepped out of the room to give us a moment. I got off the table, and my knees felt weak as I fell to the floor in tears. I felt like I'd just been punched in the gut. Matt knelt beside me, wrapped his arms around my frame, pulled me into his chest, and just kept saying, "I'm so, so sorry, honey."

"No, *I'm* sorry!" I said through tears.

On our way out, the doctor gave me an empathetic look and handed me a card with her personal phone number in case we had any questions. I got into the car in disbelief, wishing I could wake up and make it all go away. It was a dream-almost-come-true, which is a nightmare in its own way.

This kind of thing happens to other people, I thought. *I never expected it to happen to me.*

When we got home, we made our way upstairs to our bedroom and just lay there together for a while. I looked up to the ceiling and shouted, "What the heck, God?"

I'd describe that as my modern, Jordanized version of Psalm 22:2: "My God, I cry out by day, but you do not answer, by night, but I find no rest." It may sound different, but I think the question came from the same place of hurt, confusion, and despair. What were all the prayers for if they were just left unanswered?

I sent a text to my mom and a few close friends who had been praying for the appointment to let them know what happened.

I immediately started to think of all the things I could have done to cause it.

Was it the wine I had on Thanksgiving before finding out I was pregnant?

When I jumped up and down with my mom after I told her the big news?

The sushi I ate the week the baby would have been conceived?

I never knew that mom guilt could be so real even before you experience the fullness of motherhood.

I recounted every step I could remember of the previous eight weeks, trying with all my might to pinpoint exactly why this happened, searching for an answer I'd never actually find.

Then, as I lay there feeling absolutely crushed, I began to feel *bitter* toward all my friends who had seemingly perfect pregnancies and beautiful babies. When they texted me their condolences, I had to fight the urge to roll my eyes. *Psh, like you'd understand.*

I hated that I even thought such things, but I'm here to be honest, not to make myself look any better than I am.

On top of feeling just so incredibly sad and let down, I

also felt kind of silly. *Why did I get my hopes up? Why did I get our families so excited and put so much effort into telling them with special gifts? That was all for nothing and now they're let down too!*

It was almost as if I felt guilty for getting my family excited about the first grandchild they'd never get a chance to hold, especially because both my husband and I are the oldest children in our families—and for the first three years of our marriage, the only question everyone seemed to ask was "When are babies coming?"

More than anything, I felt like I'd just watched my dream to have a family be ripped away from me, only adding to my natural fears about stepping into motherhood. I didn't expect it to start off so terribly!

At the end of the long and painful physical process of the loss, I also began to feel defective, especially as I compared myself to the moms in my friend circle who had never experienced this. Compared to them, it seemed like I had failed.

In other words, I had subconsciously turned something as sacred as motherhood into something to achieve or prove I was able to do. It dawned on me that, unlike so many of the other things I'd worked to accomplish, motherhood might not be something I could just plan, control, and achieve if I only planned it out just right.

I'm sure you've felt like a failure, too, in some area. Maybe as a mom, a wife, a friend, a mentor, a businessperson, or an employee. Whether or not you *actually* failed, maybe you've experienced the sting that comes with failed plans and a shattered picture of how your hopes and dreams were *supposed* to go. Or when you've seen how that dream worked out so seamlessly for others around you, maybe you've felt you got ripped off in that department.

Unfortunately, I think we tend to tie our identity to our circumstances or experiences. At least, I know I did. Although most broken dreams, especially loss, are so far outside our control, it's almost as if something inside us defaults to owning the disrupted or destroyed plan as our own failing.

That's when we need to shift our perspective. That's when I think we could all use my mom's advice. Let me explain . . .

It Is Not a Test

While so many deep aspects of grief go far beyond the feeling of failure or disappointment that comes with a loss like this, this isn't a grief or loss book. So although there is no comparison between the pain of a devastating loss and the disappointment of unmet expectations, I want to focus on the feeling of failure that can creep up when something we hope for goes wrong (especially when nothing about it is our fault).

Most of us have had to wrestle through anger, grief, comparison, and confusion to finally get to a place of acceptance as well as a position of overcoming when something goes so sideways it breaks our hearts and makes us question everything we believed.

I certainly have had to, especially in the face of a deeper pain than I'd ever felt before. When I went through that loss, my mom came into town for a few days to make us meals and just be with me. She cleaned my house and bought me groceries, sat next to me, cried with me, and brushed the rat's nests my hair had turned into. *Bless her.*

After a few days passed and with some good old-fashioned mom prodding, she pushed me to open up about what I was thinking and how I was feeling. I didn't really know how to answer, but I admitted that I couldn't shake the feeling that I'd failed and let the whole family down.

She put her arms around me and pulled me in close. And then she said something that has stuck with me ever since: "Oh, honey, but you didn't let anyone down. You didn't fail. You want to know why?"

I sniffled. "Why?"

"Because this is not a test." She let those words sink in for a moment. "When it comes to sacred things like this, you can't pass or fail, because it is not a test. It's not something you'll get a gold medal for if it works out how you hope, and it's not something you'll be disqualified from if things don't work out exactly how you planned. If it were, *every* mom would be considered a failure, even if they had perfect pregnancies and delivered beautifully healthy babies. And that's just not the case."

She continued, "I believe that true success is not measured by how perfectly things go or the specifics of how anything works out, for that matter. The success of a mom is in how well she loves. True success in *anything* boils down to how we love. You, my dear, have given your first baby so much love. And that makes you one heckuva mom."

Cue the tears. She was right. When it comes to our greatest dream, whether that's to be a mom or grow a company or rescue children from human trafficking, *it is not a test*.

It's a *journey*. It's a *calling*.

One experience along the way—whether it goes absolutely sideways, breaks our hearts, or ends in the outcome we wanted—is not the defining factor. The true measure of our success is how well we love as we build.

And that dares me to believe that a successful life is less about achieving our greatest dreams and more about how we love and keep loving—and keep fighting and keep dreaming—even when those dreams fall apart.

Look. I know that when something good goes sideways—something that was *supposed* to be beautiful and incredible—it can be so natural to focus on how we think we failed or even let others down. I also know that disappointment, heartbreak, and feelings of utter failure aren't unique to me or to this one circumstance. It isn't an isolated experience, and those feelings come up in countless situations.

This means that, regardless of how big our dreams are or how much drive or discipline we have, we aren't immune to hardships and challenges as we build a family, a home, a business, a healthier body, a stronger marriage, a résumé, or whatever. Although the circumstances vary, our plans, hopes, and aspirations are inevitably going to get screwed up in some way at some point or another because we live in a broken world. And that's going to hurt. Sometimes it's going to hurt much worse than other times, such as in the case of an unexpected loss.

The good news? Our greatest, wildest dreams, while

things to steward with excellence, are *not* merely tests. When things don't go according to plan, we are extended the invitation to draw closer to what matters most, rediscover the depth of who we are, get back up, and continue to unapologetically pursue what we are called to do, even when we can take only one tiny step forward at a time.

The First Steps Forward

For as long as I could remember, work had motivated me. It drove me. Doing something I loved got me out of bed and ready to face each day. And that's fantastic. I wholeheartedly believe in the importance of being fulfilled by your work.

However, achievement drove me until grief outweighed the fulfillment from the work and my commitment to my professional aspirations.

Almost two weeks passed after that dreadful day at the ob-gyn, and the days felt like a blur. I just wasn't sure how to function normally again. I knew at some point I'd have to get back into the swing of things . . . but *how?*

It was so difficult to prioritize my commitments the same way I had before. In light of what I'd just experienced, work seemed wildly insignificant.

I also didn't want to jump back into my work as a way to distract myself from the emotional and physical healing that demanded my attention. I'd done that before—I'd avoided creating space for sacred, hard, and messy things by running faster, finding more to do, and making myself feel better with achievements I could control. But not this time. It just didn't seem like a viable option, nor did I really have the motivation to do that.

However, while I needed the space and time, I knew I needed to take some steps forward somehow. But I quickly realized I had *no* idea where to start. What do you do first after a blow like that? How do you get back to living your life—and *liking* your life—when it feels upside down?

I thought about how we'd have to redo all the plans we made for the year and unschedule the maternity leave I'd originally scheduled in. I mulled over these questions: *How do I just go back to business as usual? As if nothing happened? How do I still get up and give my best when it feels unimportant in comparison to what I've just experienced?*

I shared this struggle with a few trusted women in my life, and I realized I was essentially asking, *How do I move forward from here, especially if I have to move forward in a direction I never wanted to go?*

As I reflected on this question with the encouragement of trusted friends, I decided to start with one small step at a time. I didn't need to throw myself back into pursuing all the professional dreams that this major life disruption had put on pause. Going about business as usual just wouldn't be possible or healthy.

At the same time, I didn't want to just sit around and wallow for weeks on end. So I decided to try something as I inched my way back up. I decided to do one normal thing a day.

One normal thing a day.

Thinking about getting back into life slowly made taking

steps in the right direction seem achievable rather than overwhelming.

I made a list of some of the normal things I knew I could do and assigned one to each day for the upcoming five days. My normal-thing-of-the-day list looked something like this:

Monday—go for a long walk
Tuesday—write a blog post
Wednesday—respond to business emails
Thursday—go to dinner with a friend
Friday—organize office

Seeing a week scheduled with small, enjoyable steps toward getting back in the swing of things encouraged me. After I completed each one, I'd cross it off my list with a sense of accomplishment. As trite as it may sound, a few days into doing one normal thing a day, I realized I was motivated to do some other normal things too!

By Wednesday, I was feeling much more engaged with my life again, so I added a few things that weren't on my normal-thing-of-the-day agenda at all. For example, on Thursday, I also finished some administrative tasks on my to-do list and on Friday, I also managed to get laundry done and make some edits to a project I had started working on before the holidays.

As a person who used to cram my days full of things to do, it was a little weird to start with such tiny steps. But in doing so, I felt empowered and capable again. Starting with something as small and normal as going for a long walk before I felt like getting up off the couch or facing the world helped me slowly feel like myself again. In many ways, I was changed by the experience. And although the sadness didn't just disappear, I did get some of my zest for life back one small step at a time.

That experiment taught me that when I feel stuck, there is so much power in taking teeny, tiny steps forward. A little progress is better than no progress, and it's always better to start small than to not start at all.

And by the way, that applies to everything in life, not just overcoming a major heartbreak or curveball.

If you've walked through something hard and you're struggling to find the motivation to move forward, start by giving yourself permission to take the time you need. Then take small steps, even if they're so small they seem silly. If you do this, eventually you'll be dreaming and really living again.

Don't throw yourself back into business as usual right away or try to distract yourself with a million to-dos. As you feel ready or even a little bit before you feel ready, start by doing *one* normal thing a day.

Make your own one-normal-thing-a-day list for the next several days. Map out at least one normal and enjoyable thing you plan to do each day, whether that's running an errand, pulling the weeds in your garden, cooking a delicious meal, or going for a bike ride.

Your One-Step-a-Day List

On the flip side, if you haven't recently walked through a setback from illness or heartbreak but have put ambitions and dreams on the back burner for a while, perhaps because of past disappointments or fear of failure, you can implement the same concept to take ownership of these things one step at a time.

Instead of feeling like you have to "go big or go home" or "go all in" now, consider how you can move 1 percent closer to the goal you've been dreaming of.

For example, let's say you've been wanting to start a bakery for years but between your current schedule, failed attempts, and pesky fears, you're having a hard time finding any kind of motivation to do much more than daydream about it.

First ask yourself, *Why do I want to open a bakery?*

If you don't have a solid answer or your answer is kind of arbitrary such as "Well, because someone told me I'm good at baking and should start a bakery," then that may be a sign to think twice before investing time and energy in something that you don't have a clear purpose for.

However, if you have a solid answer or *why* behind that dream, such as "To support my family" or "To do something that's fulfilling to me" or "To provide people who have food allergies with delicious, gluten-free treats they can enjoy," then great—you've got a solid foundation to support what you want to do. This is your sign to proceed.

Instead of going all in, all at once, create a one-step-a-day list (or one-step-a-week list if you need to move slower). We live in a world that tells us to take massive action. However, my motto is "Incremental, implementable, imperfect action" because massive action sounds *massively overwhelming*. If you don't have the resources or the white space in your calendar to take massive action and just open a bakery tomorrow—as if that's an easy thing to do—you're likely to do nothing at all.

Too often we think that if we can't do everything, we shouldn't do *anything*. Or if our first attempts didn't work out how we hoped, it's tempting to throw in the towel altogether. Many of us don't move forward on the things we hope to do, either because our first try didn't work or because we've been told to go big or go home. But as my friend Jess Ekstrom once shared with me, "Start small at home." I love that—don't you?

As you make your one-step-a-day list, think about what small things you can do to move forward, even if you can't just open a full-blown bakery right now.

Your list might look something like this:

Day 1: Brainstorm, and put together one recipe (such as a pastry).

Day 2: Bake a batch of the recipe.

Day 3: Give samples to family and friends, ask for feedback, and perfect the recipe.

Day 4: Research local cafés and coffee shops.

Day 5: Call those shops, and offer to supply pastries for their customers.

Day 6: For those that say yes, decide how many you'll need to make each week.

Day 7: Create a sticker or packaging for your pastries so guests know they're yours.

Day 8: Develop a timeline and plan for testing your pastries in the local shops.

Of course, this is just an example, but the point is that rather than indefinitely putting off your dream, you can move in that direction at a sustainable pace and in a way that fits your needs now. You don't have to raise tens of thousands in up-front capital or start your own brick-and-mortar bakery today to take steps in the direction you know you wish to go.

Taking one step a day is a necessary discipline to achieve our dreams, because success doesn't come all at once. It comes one step at a time.

With one tiny step a day for several days (or weeks), you could be selling your pastries in coffee shops without needing to take the massive action of starting your own shop. In fact, this may be a more realistic starting point to get practice without the headache of finding and renting a store, buying equipment, hiring and managing employees, and creating all your legal policies. If you tried to start a bakery before and it didn't work out, maybe trying again without all those encumbrances could serve you well.

Those bigger steps can come later, when you're ready. In the meantime, this will give you a start on what you've been wanting to do and help you evaluate (1) whether you even like doing it as a job and (2) whether you wish to invest more time, talent, and resources to pursue it more seriously.

Maybe you've found yourself constantly putting the dream or calling in your heart on the back burner because it didn't work out in the past, because you're afraid to fail, or because something has forced you to pause the pursuit of it (such as caring for an aging parent or grieving a loss). If it's possible to pursue in this season but you're unsure where to start, create a one-step-a-day list.

Whether you need to create a one-normal-thing-a-day list to get back into the swing of life after something really hard or a one-step-a-day list to get your dream off the back burner, take some time to brainstorm what this could look like for you.

Creating and using one of these tools is a simple discipline that helped me take the time I needed without giving up on my God-given purpose just because unexpected pain messed up my plan. And I believe it can do the same for you too.

Above all, when life hands you hardship or your dreams don't go according to plan, revisit *why* you're pursuing whatever it is that you are. Then give yourself permission to dream again and to keep going when you get stuck, even if you have to start small and move slow, one step at a time.

4

Always Almost There

I recently listened to a voice message from a friend. In it, she shared something that stood out to me: "I always feel like I'm *almost* where I want to be."

She went on to say that no matter how much she tried, she felt as though she lacked essential resources to get to the next level in her business. She'd tried all the strategies, but it seemed like she didn't have either the time or the team to get to where she felt she should be. I responded, sharing how much I understood the feeling and pointed to specific examples of when I felt I'd plateaued or chased what felt like a moving target in one thing or another.

She sent back a text: "It's frustrating because it seems like I'm doing the same thing as all these other people I see absolutely crushing it. I'm doing all the right things. And I don't know if they're breezing through milestones easily because they have some secret strategy that I haven't yet uncovered—although I believe I'm familiar with all of them—or are simply more organized and disciplined than me."

This led to a long conversation about abundance versus scarcity, the pursuit of more, and whether we were really as behind or stuck as it might seem. We discussed how an abundance mindset can see all the good in our lives, whereas a scarcity mindset always tells us that what we have or what we're pursuing will never be enough.

Do you ever believe the lie that when you get "here" or "there," you'll finally be successful—only to realize you might be chasing a moving target? Ever feel like you're *always almost* where you want to be? Or as though the second you reach a milestone, everyone around you has already moved past it and there's another thing to achieve? As though you're always playing keep-up or catch-up and never quite content with where you are?

Maybe you have a three-bedroom house but now find yourself feeling like you need a four-bedroom. Perhaps you feel like you've plateaued in your career or business and, no matter what you try, you just can't break through to that next level, where you thought you'd be by now. You have the talent, the energy, and the experience . . . but something just hasn't clicked into place to make it possible (at least, not yet).

You may be dealing with this struggle in a different area entirely. But I'm sure you're familiar with the feeling of nothing ever quite being enough. Just when you think you're close, the finish line seems to move.

The conversation with my friend reminded me of a meeting I'd had with my husband about a year earlier. It brought back to mind the principles we discussed, many of which I was able to share with her. I'd like to share some of these principles with you too.

How Much Is Enough?

To get the full visual, picture me sitting in my office, wearing slippers and holey sweatpants (because I'm fancy like that), working on our business and personal financial goals with my husband. It was mid-February, about a month after our loss. Since the year hadn't started out the way we planned and since I no longer had to take a maternity leave the upcoming August, we had to revisit the calendar as well as the financial projections for the remainder of the year.

Matt pointed to a project I had mapped out on a whiteboard. "What about this project? What's the revenue goal?"

I thought for a second and threw out a pretty large number.

In the moment, I fully expected him to write that number on the board and start reverse engineering how we'd achieve that goal, like we normally do.

But he didn't. He didn't say whether that goal was right or wrong either. He simply challenged me: "Okay. I believe that's absolutely possible . . . but I'm curious—*why* is that your goal?"

Why? Uh . . . I don't know. I just pulled that number out of the blue. I heard a colleague sharing that she recently made that much on a project, and it sounds like a good goal to aim for.

I admitted those thoughts out loud and then said, "I don't know exactly why, but I think I thought that if we hit that number, I'd be able to hire the additional team members I've wanted to bring on as my publishing and podcasting careers are growing."

"Okay," he answered. "That's fair. But you've just been through a lot, and I think it's important to keep your stress levels low. I don't want to see you go through another year of hustle and burnout without even knowing *what we actually need* in order to do those things."

He continued, "It's not wrong to have big goals or even to make more than we need if that's how things work out, but I think it's unhealthy for us to push for that just for the sake of doing something that *sounds* good. Instead, I think we need to approach our goals by asking 'Why?' about each one. From there, we can get specific and define *enough* for ourselves for the time period we're looking at. That way, we don't burn out trying to go at an unsustainable pace. We've done that before, and we don't need to do it again."

Thank You, Lord, for a logical, rational husband who never shames or doubts my big goals but also brings me back to earth when I start chasing them arbitrarily.

He dug deeper. "Tell me, *Why* do you want to hire more team members?"

"A few reasons," I said. "Well, like you said, it's important to me to reduce my stress levels and get out of the weeds. Plus, through everything we just experienced, I've developed an even deeper appreciation for being able to work from home and have flexibility in my schedule. I'd love to provide opportunities like that for other women so they can provide for their households and have flexibility too," I explained as I thought of the Proverbs 31 woman.

"Bingo," he said. "Now we've got a clear mission to drive what we're doing. Next we need to get clear on how much money we *actually* need to move the needle in that direction this year."

So we opened a big spreadsheet, wrote down our personal financial goals, then looked at the business needs. We estimated how much we'd budget for each role I wanted to hire as well as the investing we wanted to do. Know what we found?

After looking at how that project fit into the bigger picture, we realized that I needed to make only about *half* as much as I thought I did to achieve those goals. This allowed me to take a deep breath—a sigh of relief. The pressure drastically decreased simply by asking "Why?" and examining our goals a little more closely.

For so long I thought I needed to make a kajillion dollars to do the things I hoped to do. This led me to hustle my butt off and chase massive goals without knowing what I actually *needed* financially to achieve them.

As I saw that day, what I could do instead was start with my aim in mind, get clear on the resources I truly needed, prepare accordingly, and then ensure that those resources were allocated properly.

"How much is enough?" is a question we all need to be asking. Coincidentally, I've found that it's usually in the face of unmet expectations or heartbreak that I'm dared to take this question seriously. When something goes wrong or knocks us down, I think there's an internal switch that flips and causes us to focus on the essentials: *What is the priority, and how much of a given resource (time, money, etc.) do I need to pursue that?*

When we're not challenged by the pain of disappointment or almost-but-not-quite moments, it can be so easy to get caught up in all the possibilities without having a clear priority. So, in a strange and beautiful way, the wounds from our deepest disappointments and devastating experiences can serve as defining moments that help us look past arbitrary pressure and define what *enough* looks like in our lives.

Define *Enough* by Asking "Why?"

One of the most important things we can do in the face of unmet expectations and almost-but-not-quite moments is to accept their (often painfully delivered) invitation to ask "Why?" so that we aren't driven by vanity, comparison, or the pressure to achieve something for the sake of achievement. This is especially true when we feel the need to reach for accomplishment or accolades that almost seem to make up for whatever it is that hasn't gone right in our lives.

In other words, when we lean into the fact that we don't need to do everything to be happy and instead choose to believe that our deepest losses and letdowns don't define us, we can start to invest our efforts in a more intentional way. By doing so, we can create a lovely existence full of things that matter, make an impact on others without overextending ourselves, and steward the life right in front of us well.

This often starts with defining *enough*.

The discipline of defining *enough* requires auditing each

commitment, task, and goal that takes up space on our plates by asking, "Why? Why am I doing or pursuing this?"

Instead of hustling nonstop and driving ourselves into the ground, we'd be wise to set meaningful, clear goals based on our needs, what we currently have, and our overarching purpose.

All too often we set unrealistic and even unnecessary goals, and as I have learned the hard way, that can lead to hustle and burnout.

Prior to pregnancy and loss, it was common for me to set lofty goals for myself. I thought having enough meant getting more, more, and more. Many of my goals, especially financial goals, were chosen based on what I thought sounded good or what I heard other people saying *their* goals were. While I can still overextend myself if I'm not careful (ahem, see my failed project from the first chapter), my experience prompted me to look at my goals through the lens of what matters most and start making changes to my approach.

Examine your own life and goal setting. For example, have you ever wanted to lose ten pounds because your sister did? Don't get me wrong. It's great to be inspired and positively influenced by someone else. However, if you asked yourself why you wanted to lose weight and the only reason you came up with was "Well, my sister did it, so I need to as well," you might have a hard time sticking to your commitment.

Why is that? I'd argue it's because when we're not clear on what we actually need or don't have a deeper meaning driving our goals, we may have a more difficult time sticking with them. Plus, if you're setting goals based on what *sounds* good or on what you see other people do, you may not actually be pursuing the right goals for you.

When we set a goal for an arbitrary or shallow reason, we may find that the thing we're investing energy in isn't even aligned with our own priorities or needs.

On the flip side, a deeper, more lasting purpose may be driving your ambition, such as "I want to lose weight because I know that taking care of my health now improves my odds of being healthy and available for my family in the future." That's a purpose worth pursuing, right? Focusing on something bigger than yourself grounds your goal in the stewardship of your actual values rather than in comparison or vanity.

So, if you were to evaluate your own health needs, rather than arbitrarily setting a weight-loss goal because of your sister's journey, you might find that you should aim to lose only five pounds. Or you might find that you need to lose fifteen pounds to be your healthiest self and to fulfill the deeper *why* behind what you're about to pursue.

Allow me to give you another example to consider. In the business world, it's common to hear about the six-figure milestone, as if once you get to six figures, you've made it to the mystical land of success. Once you hit six figures, the goal becomes to hit seven figures. And it just goes on and on. Trust me—I've learned by experience that I can feel a lot more satisfied making much less if I'm creating a life I enjoy and not just chasing more for the sake of more.

In other words, a single number, milestone, or achievement doesn't equal success, nor does it mean that you'll be fulfilled, present, and available for what matters most.

You can manage to make seven figures or more and still be utterly miserable, burned out, or disconnected from what's most important to you. Your motivation can't be the milestone or the goal itself. It must be the *why*, the purpose behind what you're doing, for it to be sustainable and worthwhile. This makes the goal you're aiming for less like a trophy to show off and more like a vehicle to help you achieve that purpose. After all, that satisfaction lasts only for a second before someone else has something even more impressive to show.

If you determine you need $1 million to fulfill the *why* you've decided on, then great—that money will serve as a vehicle to carry out the mission. But if a clear mission isn't tied to the dollars and cents, the arbitrary pursuit of more will likely only create more stress. While more isn't bad, more isn't always better. The right milestone or goal will vary for each one of us depending on our priorities and what we need to fulfill our purpose in one season or another.

My friend and I shared some of these thoughts as we texted, and they convicted me again almost a whole year after my conversation with Matt during our financial planning meeting. In fact, in sharing these thoughts with my friend, I was challenged to take inventory of ways I might have lost sight of them myself. Coincidentally, this text conversation happened just weeks after my "failed" launch that I mentioned in the first chapter. Needless to say, sometimes it takes various experiences to really get the lesson through my hard head. Hashing out these all-too-common feelings with a trusted friend, as well as reflecting on all that my husband and I had discussed the year before, led me to take an intentional sabbatical from pursuing growth or setting new goals.

As the summer months approached, I decided I would take three months off from trying to grow my business and instead use that time to focus on stewarding and optimizing what I already had. I thought that perhaps part of the reason I rarely felt satisfied was that I have the tendency to achieve a goal and set a new one immediately afterward without taking much time to celebrate or appreciate whatever I just achieved. So I decided to take a small window of time to let all that I had already done be enough without pushing toward the next goal. And those three months were transformative for me. I went from hearing the constant whisper in the back of my mind say, *You're not there yet* or *You're still behind,* to looking around at my work and my life and saying, "Today this is enough."

So, what's my point? It's important to regularly ask ourselves critical questions like, *Why that number, goal, or level?* and *Is that what I actually need to get to where I want to or need to go? Or does it just sound sexy?*

If we asked those types of questions more often, we might find that we need less or that we're aiming too low or—like I did when I happened to be texting about this with my friend—that we're actually exactly where we need to be.

In order to define *enough* and pursue the right goals for ourselves, especially when life tosses us a curveball or knocks us down, we have to ask the following questions:

- *What do I hope to achieve?*
- *Why do I want to achieve that? Why am I doing what I'm doing?*
- *How will I get there? What will I need to reach that goal?*

If you've been pursuing something for a while now or you've recently faced a disappointment or setback, this is your invitation to reevaluate all that's on your plate. Do you like what's there? Does anything need to change? Look at each goal and commitment and then look back to why you started in the first place to determine whether the goals you're aiming for are still in alignment with that purpose.

For the ones that are, define what enough looks like for you and make a plan to steward those things with excellence and focus.

For any that are not, stop looking around at everyone else. Instead, narrow your focus, refine your goals based on *your* needs, and then consider how you will pursue them from a place of purpose rather than out of the pressure to prove something to people who have their own lives to worry about.

And remember, defining *enough* is in no way settling or playing small. It's fighting for contentment in a world that constantly tells us never to be content and that if we're content, it must mean we're complacent. Nothing could be further from the truth. Complacency and contentment are two different mindsets entirely. The former lacks direction and intention. The latter is full of both.

Choosing to define *enough*—to pursue what you care

about and actually need—isn't the easy way out. In a culture of "never enough," it's a way to swim upstream. Truth be told, not only is it important when faced with almosts and unknowns, but it's also the very discipline we need when it comes to our daily thriving and building lives we really, truly like.

5

When Things Don't Go According to Plan (Again)

You know those times when you get thrown off course and, just when you've almost caught your breath and you've started to move forward with a new plan, something wrecks those plans as well? Me too.

I was on my way to an event in mid-March 2020, preparing to give a keynote in front of six thousand college students. Matt chose to come with me. Unfortunately, no direct flights were available, and with connections and layovers, it would have taken us longer to fly than drive, so we chose to brave a long road trip together.

We were about three-quarters of the way there when a friend texted me, "Are you still going to speak with the whole world going crazy?"

I read the text out loud. "What does she mean?" I knew the COVID-19 virus had begun to hit the United States, but I hadn't heard anything to suggest the whole world was "going crazy." I looked at Matt. "Is it really that bad?"

At Matt's shrug, I turned back to my phone and texted, "I'm not paying too much attention to the news, but we're still on as of now."

Five minutes later, I saw a notification on social media. I'd been tagged by the organization that I was scheduled to speak for the following morning. The post was promotional, highlighting me as the keynote speaker. But the comments were what drew my attention. They were full of concerned students essentially protesting the event.

Not exactly a nice, warm welcome.

I began to read through them, and as I did, I got my first taste of the world "going crazy."

> "The governor just banned large social gatherings in
> the state! This should be canceled!"
> "Do you want us all to get sick and die?"
> "Doesn't the administration realize what's going on
> in the world? No large gatherings!"
> "They canceled March Madness. Why isn't *this*
> canceled?"

I reread that last one. *They canceled March Madness? Can they do that? Is that allowed?*

Comments like these prompted me to do a little intel (aka googling) about what was going on.

Like I said, I'd heard about COVID-19 prior to this road trip, but no one seemed too concerned about it until, all of a sudden, everyone panicked. There wasn't much of a transition either. One day we were all pretty chill. *Psh, no big deal. It's not that serious.* The next day they closed down Disney and practically everything else in the country.

We continued to our destination, but after arriving in town that night, we learned that the in-person event was going to be canceled. Instead, I'd give a virtual presentation that would be livestreamed. I had been looking forward to that presentation for months, and although not a catastrophe compared to the bigger things happening in the world, it felt like a major letdown, especially after driving all that way!

While it wasn't the original plan, we made it work. By the time we arrived back home the following evening, the president had declared a national state of emergency and the governor had enacted a two-week stay-at-home order.

Just like everyone else, I wasn't sure what to make of it. The only thing I knew was that my plans were about to be flipped upside down again. I began to wonder whether there was any point to planning out my year in the first place . . .

When One Plan After Another
Falls Apart

A few days later, after thoroughly freaking out and stress-eating a pint of ice cream, I collected myself and called a meeting with my small team. We had scheduled a pretty big project to launch a couple of weeks later and needed to discuss an alternative plan of action.

It struck me that we were about to lose a lot of money and time that we had invested in this project. We had almost (but not quite) seen a new plan through, and now things were going sideways. That meant we had to adapt our plan, and we gathered virtually over a video call to discuss our options.

After the loss I'd experienced a few months earlier, we'd already had to rework our plans for the year. And now something else had come up and ruined those plans too.

Ugh. It was so maddening.

I didn't see it in that frustrating and stressful moment, but I see it now: in those back-to-back experiences that forced me to replan a year twice within the first quarter, I was learning how to release control in ways I hadn't had to before.

I often say that the most important lessons are the hardest to learn, and both delayed and disrupted dreams have only solidified that belief in me. Some lessons—the ones that rub against the very grain of our being—come the hard way as we learn how to adapt and make the most of the circumstances we face.

I wonder whether perhaps some of those experiences were not merely inconveniences but also invitations to trust God and grow in a way I might otherwise have missed, had I still been under the illusion that if I just planned enough or did enough, I would maintain full control.

To be clear, I absolutely loathe feeling out of control. I enjoy knowing exactly how things are going to go and getting to choose what I will do. I had already experienced that out-of-control feeling with my loss. Once was enough for the year, thank you very much.

Although I wouldn't voluntarily sign up for this kind of out-of-control situation again, I've since seen the way unexpected good things sprout out of my ability to be adaptable.

For one thing, this situation helped me learn the benefits of planning in shorter increments. It also dared me to open my hands, release even just a tiny bit of control, and learn new ways to problem-solve.

Additionally, I was again forced to reassess my goals and dreams.

Which of these projects and goals are truly necessary? Which are aligned with where I want to go, and which are not?

As we pivoted, I began to think more critically about what I wanted to push forward on versus what I needed to pause. What would best serve my team, my life, my family, and my community amid these unexpected circumstances?

When it comes to our hopes, plans, ambitions, and dreams, the reality is that we have control over only a few key things: *what* we choose to focus on next, *why* we choose the things that we do, and *how* we respond when plans work out and when they don't.

Okay, okay. That sounds great and all, but can I be honest? I don't often think much about my response in the moment that something goes wrong. I just react—sometimes emotionally. Sometimes I eat a pint of ice cream, for heaven's sake. Real losses and letdowns come with *real* implications. So when plans fall apart, I don't generally just think logically or have a cool, calm, and collected response—at least not immediately. I'm not a robot, after all. Instead, I'm more likely to spiral downward as I ask every hard question I can think of: *Why is this happening? What am I supposed to do now?* Only after I process all the emotions that the situation brings up can I collect myself and respond well.

So, if you're a human, too, the best encouragement I can

offer you is to give yourself the grace and space to acknowledge the fears, frustrations, and other feelings that come up when you're faced with setbacks or disappointments. Then, once you freak out for a minute, take a deep breath and ask yourself, *What's the best next step I can take? How can I make the most of this almost?*

Looking back now, more than a year later, I can see that those disruptions that forced me to replan led to some good things for both my work and me personally. Because I was willing to adapt—okay, I was forced into it—I did fewer projects but ultimately felt I accomplished more meaningful work than ever because I wasn't spread too thin.

And I can't help but think that was a gift I never asked for but truly needed.

Navigating the Unpredictable

Let's face it. *All* seasons are unpredictable. Our next almost-but-not-quite experience could be just around the corner at any given moment. Of course, some hold more variables than others, but each can present its own set of challenges to navigate. It turns out that school didn't prepare us for everything life could throw our way—like pregnancy loss, lost profits, and pandemics.

But what I've learned is that even when things *seem* steady and secure, it's wise not to fall under the illusion that we're in full control. Are there choices within our control? *Of course.* Can we make our lives better or worse based on the choices we make? *Most of the time.* However, countless factors are so beyond our control that even our best efforts might land us just short of the finish line of our plans or goals. When we accept that very little is truly stable, we are best equipped to handle unmet expectations and broken plans with adaptability.

With that in mind, I want to share a couple of key lessons that have helped me navigate unexpected interruptions and unmet expectations. Whether or not you're also a planner by nature, these steps can soften the blow when no matter what you try, things just don't go according to plan.

Plan in Shorter Increments

During my meeting with my team as the lockdowns began, I knew I needed to approach planning differently. So rather than trying to replan an entire year for the third time while facing a very uncertain future, we focused on planning the next ninety days—and *only* the next ninety days. Given how the previous few months had gone, it would be a waste of energy to try to make a picture-perfect plan for the remainder of the year.

Through this exercise, I've found that planning in monthly or quarterly increments helps me stay focused and remain flexible. I used to plan my entire year, but twelve months is a lot of time for things—circumstances, priorities, capacity, the world around me—to change drastically. When I expect a whole year to go according to plan, I end up grasping for control instead of effectively stewarding what's right in front of me.

That's not to say that establishing goals for the whole

year isn't wise. In fact, I'd argue that it is. However, planning out every detail of an upcoming twelve-month period really only set me up for frustration and disappointment in the face of unmet expectations. Now I plan in quarters. I may forecast possibilities for the future beyond that, but I try not to set in stone anything beyond the ninety days in front of me, and even that stone is often more like wet cement.

My advice? Set a few goals, but as much as possible, plan the details for achieving them in shorter increments of time. You might find that you're able to be more focused and intentional in that shorter window and less dependent on your expectations for the future. This approach nicely blends the wisdom of planning with the freedom and whimsy of taking life one day at a time.

Focus on Doing Less but Better

As my small team discussed moving forward, we also agreed to focus on just a couple of things. For example, for the upcoming ninety days, we planned to focus on only two projects, one new and one ongoing. The ongoing project was my podcast, and the new project was a set of workshops that we believed would serve my community with the new needs they had amid all the changes thanks to COVID-19.

Rather than trying to make up for the lost revenue and almost-achieved goals by trying to do all the things, we decided to focus on doing just two things really, really well.

I've learned the hard way that experiencing true contentment and living in a way that aligns with our personal vision of success requires that we *focus*. When our ambitions start to carry us away and we try to force something to work out when plans need to change—or we pursue a million dreams at once—we will fail to do anything well. The unpredictability that we face in life highlights the importance of focusing on very few things at a time and doing them well.

This applies to more than just professional plans too. For example, if you planned to improve your health, maybe you believed you had to go all in, all at once. In our all-or-nothing world, it can feel like you need to sign up for fitness classes, eat more vegetables, get on supplements, sleep eight hours a night, and cut out sugar, caffeine, and practically everything else. And *now*. That's a lot of things.

And, hey, you might be able to sustain it for a little while. But if life happens and an unexpected disruption slows you down or makes doing *all the things* more difficult, you might feel discouraged. You might even be tempted to give up altogether.

Instead of going all in, all at once, only to consider quitting when real life hits, consider one or two changes you can focus on until they become second nature, or *habits*. Could you focus on fitness classes and reducing stress for the next ninety days? Then add in another change after a few months? This approach will help you steward the garden of your health without feeling like you're forcing it to happen in a way that isn't even manageable or enjoyable in the first place.

When we can focus without our plates being so full, we have more capacity to be flexible. In other words, we can adjust our approach without throwing in the towel when circumstances change.

Life will almost always throw a curveball—or two or twelve—when we least expect it. If we keep our hands clenched around our plans, that curveball will hit us square between the eyes and knock us out. But if we leave a little space for unexpected change, plan in smaller increments, and remain focused on doing the most important things well, we might even be able to hit that curveball.

If you remember nothing else, remember this: Plan away, but keep your hands open to change. Because success isn't just when things work out exactly how we planned; it's also when we tend to what's right in front of us even when our plans don't go according to plan.

6

When a Dream Come True Becomes a Nightmare Loop

It was an early morning in April, just a few months after our loss. I stood in my bathroom, staring at another positive pregnancy test.

I fell to my knees. "Oh, thank You, Jesus!" I whispered.

After telling Matt and then celebrating over a video call with our families, I called my doctor. She had me come in right away to get blood work done. To my relief, my levels came back looking good. I breathed a huge sigh of relief.

Aside from some major cravings, fatigue, and on-and-off nausea, the first trimester proceeded rather uneventfully. I had ultrasounds every two weeks to monitor progress and put my mind at ease, and everything appeared to be progressing perfectly.

The scan at eleven weeks showed our baby's arms, legs, hands, and feet wiggling around. We could even spot the little nose and chin. It finally started to feel real, and I felt my guard coming down.

Later that day, an early-summer storm rolled in. After it passed, Matt and I saw a perfect rainbow over the field just in front of our house. Matt ran inside and grabbed the ultrasound photos. "Go stand under the rainbow and hold this! I want to get a photo of you with our rainbow baby under the rainbow!" (For context, they call the baby who comes after a loss a "rainbow baby" because it is like a blessing after the storm.)

My heart nearly exploded with happiness as I turned to the side, placed one hand under the tiny bump that had begun to form, and held the ultrasound in the other hand. This was just too picture perfect, like a sign from God that it would all work out this time.

After we headed back inside, I looked at Matt and said, "You know, for the first time, I really believe everything is going to be okay."

He smiled at me. "That's what I've been saying! I'm so glad you think so too."

When the Dream Shatters Again

Have you ever felt stuck in a loop—as if every time your dream almost comes true, your greatest fears do instead? I have. And it's the worst.

At my twelfth week of pregnancy, we had a photo shoot with our most recent ultrasound photos so that we could make an announcement on social media the following week. The day before we planned to tell the world our big news, we had another checkup on our little one, where we would listen for the heartbeat with the Doppler. Matt had his phone out to record the precious sound as I lay on the table confidently, excited to hear it.

A minute or so passed, and I noticed the nurse's brow was furrowed as she tried to find it.

"I'm sure it's fine," she said. "Maybe I'm not doing it right. Let me grab the doctor to try with an ultrasound."

Could we really be in this situation again? No way. The scan will show us everything is okay. It has to.

A few minutes later, the doctor herself wheeled the ultrasound machine in and began the scan. That's when I knew something must be wrong. Matt stood next to me as we all squinted at the screen, looking for any sign of life.

The baby's body was bigger than the last scan but motionless. There was no movement or flicker of the heartbeat that we'd seen a few weeks earlier.

My heart sank. *This can't be happening again!*

I held my breath and waited for the doctor to confirm the news I dreaded most: I'd lost *another* baby—this time one I'd carried for three months. That's a long time to bond with your unborn baby. We'd already taken announcement photos, my mom and a close friend had already begun to plan my baby shower, and I'd let my guard down and allowed myself to love—to be vulnerable. In that moment, I regretted ever getting excited or letting myself believe everything would be okay.

With tears streaming down my cheeks, I gathered my things, and Matt and I bolted out the front door of the doctor's office, passing all the happy pregnant ladies in the waiting room.

As we pulled into our driveway, both of us in tears, I thought, *We're stuck in a nightmare loop.*

I stormed out of the car and collapsed in the backyard, shouting up to the sky, "Why? What about the rainbow, God? What about that? Why would You do that?"

If you haven't experienced this, it may sound dramatic. But it truly felt as if my whole world was falling apart. A mash-up of grief, hormones, and shock made the next couple of days an absolute blur. I found myself so angry and confused yet without a way to get the feelings out. I normally process hard things by going for a long run or doing some sort of exercise. Unfortunately, because of the physical element of what I was experiencing, running wasn't an option.

In this case, the only way I knew to release any of my feelings without causing any serious harm was by smashing old plates on the concrete. So that's what I did. The night before I went in for a D&C surgery that I could barely believe I would need to have, I opened my kitchen cabinets and found a few old turquoise plates I'd never liked much anyway. I grabbed them off the shelf, walked out to my front porch, and, with tears filling my eyes, threw them onto the concrete as I let out a sound I can only describe as a roar.

Each plate shattered the second it hit the pavement, and turquoise ceramic shards covered the sidewalk in front of me.

Did I look like a lunatic to my neighbors? Yes, probably.

Did I care in that moment? Nope.

When crap hits the fan, when pain sears through every fiber of your being, you really don't care about what people think of you.

Call me crazy, but I think there was something symbolic about it too. I stared down at the shards—broken pieces that seemed to accurately represent my mama heart, my hopes, and my dreams—in absolute disbelief.

What do you do when life breaks your heart over and over again? When, instead of getting what you've prayed for, you end up feeling more like a shattered mess on the floor?

Maybe, in a world that tells us to pull ourselves together and get on with life, we need to start with acknowledging that we are hurting, broken, and not okay.

A few weeks later, when I began seeing a therapist to work through my trauma (I've left out most of the details of that trauma to minimize possible triggers), she validated my decision to smash plates, explaining that the healthiest way to gain strength and move forward is by acknowledging the emotion we're experiencing and letting it out in a healthy way. Otherwise, it will only come out later in other, often-unhealthy ways that can harm relationships or other important parts of our lives.

Story of My Life

Lying in bed the day after surgery, I looked at Matt as he put some laundry away across the room. "I need to get out of here."

The room, the blanket, the familiarity of my own home just seemed to suffocate me, reminding me of what I'd lost and couldn't get back.

"All right," he responded, phone in hand. "Where do you want to go?"

I thought for a moment.

"I don't know . . . Montana?" I suggested, half kidding, half serious.

Within seconds, he began looking up routes to drive from our hometown in Indiana to Big Sky Country, as well as Airbnbs in Montana. To be clear, that wasn't a short drive from our home. At all.

I rolled over and let out a sigh as I realized I'd just had surgery less than twenty-four hours before. "Maybe we should stop somewhere closer to home on the way to see how I feel first."

After scrolling through endless options, we decided to check out Lake Geneva in Wisconsin, booked a two-night stay at an inn on the lake, and began to pack our bags.

We arrived just before dusk that evening, then walked out on the pier and watched the sunset as the docked boats in the marina rocked from side to side.

After resting at the lake a few days, we checked out of our hotel, hopped in the car, and started driving west toward Montana. About four hours into our drive, we stopped at a gas station somewhere in Minnesota.

While Matt pumped the gas, something came over me. I suddenly felt strongly that we shouldn't drive the rest of the way, although we had already booked and paid for an Airbnb.

I debated with myself for a minute before saying anything to my outdoorsy husband, who was very much looking forward to a week off the grid in wide-open spaces.

It'll be fun, I tried to tell my doubts.

My doubts fired back, *Yes, but you just had a pretty invasive surgery a few days ago, and you don't know how your body is going to heal. Driving all that way may not be good for you just yet.*

I countered, *It'll be good for my heart too.*

My doubts pushed back on that as well. *The doctor said your healing process will take about two weeks. It would probably be better not to be too far from home just in case any complications arise.*

I knew that complications from a D&C were rare, and none of the women I knew who had had one ever shared that they had any problems, which meant that the likelihood of anything bad happening was probably low.

Still, the doubts lingered, pestering me to say something to Matt as he pulled the car out of the gas station lot.

After working up the courage to possibly frustrate a man who had already driven over four hours, I spoke up just before he turned back onto the highway. "Babe, I don't think we should go to Montana."

He glanced over at me, surprised. "What? What do you mean? Why not?"

I shared the concerns that I had and tried to communicate where my sudden change of heart was coming from.

"I just don't know what to do," I tried to explain, "but as we get farther away from home, I feel more and more anxious. I just have a feeling in my gut that it may be best to stay closer to home a little longer since I'm only a few days post-op."

I could tell he was slightly frustrated, but he tried not to let it show. Instead, he pulled off the road into a little gravel parking lot so we could discuss our options and decide on a plan of action.

First he called the Airbnb to see whether there was any chance of being able to cancel last minute and get refunded. Of course, the answer was no, so we went back and forth, exploring our options, and spent a solid thirty minutes debating whether it would be worth it to have peace of mind and forfeit the money.

"What if we just go back to Lake Geneva for a few more days?" I suggested. "That's only a few hours from home, and I'd feel better being there than all the way across the country."

After some time, we concluded it would be best to prioritize my health and mental well-being, given the circumstances. So he put the car in drive and pulled a U-turn to head back toward the land of cheese.

It was evident that he was bummed and even a little frustrated as we realized that we had just driven four hours only to turn around and drive four hours back.

I commented, "Well, isn't that just the story of our lives lately? Starting a journey toward something we hoped for, only to have it cut short and turn around and go back to square one?"

"Ha!" he said as he grabbed my hand. "You're not kidding, girl. But we're in this together, wherever we go."

We arrived back in Lake Geneva shortly after sunset, checked into the hotel again, and decided to sit on the patio and order some drinks and appetizers after a long day of driving.

As we sat there processing the day, I realized something that you might also relate to. Similar to the half journey we'd just taken toward Montana, both times I started down the road toward motherhood, the journey began relatively easily, only to be painfully cut short, and I had to turn around and go back to the starting point with seemingly nothing to show for it.

Has something like that ever happened to you? Maybe you haven't suffered tragic loss, but maybe you have started on the road toward a milestone or desired destination, but then you were forced to turn around and start over. *Isn't it the most maddening experience?* It can feel like being stuck in a nightmare loop.

Maybe your Montana—your desired destination—is a life where you're married to your soul mate. Except every time you begin a relationship that seems promising, he becomes passive or a breakup blindsides you, just when you thought things would finally work out how you hope. Instead, you find yourself not only heartbroken but also back at square one in dating . . . again.

Or maybe your Montana is a life where you love your career. Perhaps you've tried to start a small business a handful of times, but every time you start, you run straight into a brick wall: not enough customers, not enough time, not enough money, or just not enough confidence. Rather than getting to the place you hoped you'd be, with a thriving full-time business, you find yourself back at the starting line . . . again.

Perhaps your Montana is a healthier, pain-free life. You've worked with a million doctors and been tested for just about everything possible. Every time you try a new nutrition or treatment regimen, you see *some* progress, but the relief is temporary and you end up right back where you started . . . again.

Maybe your Montana—that life you're longing for—looks like something else entirely. But I think we all have our Montanas, our visions of the life we truly want.

When we keep having to turn around just when we *almost* get to where we're going, our feelings can range from disappointment to utter despair.

I should clarify something—I think we can all agree that some experiences are more devastating than others. Some may be deeper or more life altering. However, I share a range of examples because, even with very different experiences, we can all connect on the frustration of getting *almost* where we wanted to be, only to have something come along and force us to start over.

So, my question becomes, How do we keep finding the courage to try again when the long journey makes us start over at square one? How do we keep believing when the desired destination—our Montana—seems so far away?

I wish there were an easy, three-step answer to those complex questions. But if that very inefficient road trip taught me anything worth sharing, it's this: on the way to your greatest dreams, don't count on a straight shot.

Don't Count on a Straight Shot

The journey to our most precious dreams and all that we were made to be—whether that's a mom, a wife, a leader, a professional athlete, or something else—is almost never a straight shot or a smooth road. It's not even a windy or bumpy road. For most of us, it involves U-turns, detours, and redirections. I look back on many of the dreams I've pursued—getting married and becoming an author, for example—and see that the road I took to those things had twists, turns, bumps, and detours too. Not a single one of those experiences was a straight path from point A to point B, and many required starting back at square one just before it all would have come together.

For example, when my husband and I were engaged, he was pursuing his own dream of playing in the NFL. In a way, I felt as though I was pursuing the dream with him. To our dismay, the process was not at all like we see on TV. You know, where first-round draft picks get a call, sign a multimillion-dollar contract, and seem to live happily ever after. Yeah, it's not always like that. A lot happens both before and after a contract is signed—and a lot of it is disappointment and shattered dreams. The process put both Matt and me—and our plans for our life—on an unpredictable roller coaster for a while. He got a workout but didn't get signed. Then he eventually got another workout and did get signed. He even got a jersey printed with his last name and played in a preseason game, giving us a taste of the dream come true. Then, just when it looked like everything was going according to plan, he was released.

Needless to say, planning a wedding around those ever-changing circumstances wasn't exactly a walk in the park, and we ended up having a longer-than-intended engagement and scheduling three different wedding dates *and* three different wedding venues before we finally tied the knot on the third date and venue, ironically on the third of the month. A few months later, Matt was scheduled to attend a pretty important camp to showcase his skills. Scouts would be there, and going would increase his chances of getting picked up by another team. Well, not long before the camp, he began to feel intense pain in his abdomen and ended up having an emergency appendectomy. After his surgery, the doctor told us he couldn't exercise or lift anything over ten pounds for four to six weeks. *Well, there goes the camp,* we thought. Although there was nothing fun about it at the time, that messy season full of letdowns, rejections, and unknowns helped us redefine our dreams. We were dared to ask, "What do we really want for our lives, and is the NFL the only way to create the life we long for?"

In other words, would another career path still allow us to get to where we were going? As it turned out, the NFL wasn't the only way, and now I'm grateful for those days.

For a while, we had viewed Matt making it in the NFL as the desired destination, our Montana, if you will. However, as we began to consider what we really valued, we realized our true desired destination wasn't the specific experience of having a jersey with his name on it. Instead, the dream was the life that football appeared to create—a life where we had flexibility, enjoyed our work, could make a positive impact on others, and were involved in a like-minded community.

The more we thought about it, the more we saw that a career in the NFL was a route we could take, but it wasn't the ultimate destination. There were plenty of other ways to create a life full of those things, and that's when we began to pursue entrepreneurship. It's also when we decided to join a church community as well as business masterminds. Within just a few years, we found that we had the flexibility we hoped for, enjoyed our work, were able to donate to causes we believed in, and were plugged into the like-minded community we desired.

The original route we set out on might not have taken us where we expected, but we've paved a way and created a life that works for us. It might not have worked out how *we* pictured, but that doesn't mean *God's* plan didn't work out exactly how it was supposed to.

Similarly, in my writing career, I've experienced my fair share of U-turns. The first time I pitched a book proposal to publishers, each one said no. I thought that maybe I'd gotten my dream wrong—that maybe I wasn't cut out to write a book. But then, with some encouragement from friends, I decided not to try to force being traditionally published. Instead, I self-published a short devotional-style book and focused on speaking to develop my message. To my surprise, just over a year later, when I wasn't even looking, an editor reached out to me via email. After several conversations, I got an opportunity to write my first book, *Own Your Everyday*. Even that book wasn't written and published without several restarts and rewrites that made it the bestselling book it became.

Although these are obviously much lighter examples than the story I opened the chapter with, I share this to make an important point. Many of the most precious things until this point in my life haven't come fast or easy. Most have been refined—or redefined—through the fire of rejections, restarts, and redirections.

In fact, I'd argue that it's a huge, unexpected blessing when things *do* work out beautifully on the first try, because that's rare. That doesn't make it hurt any less when our journey is cut short, but I do believe it brings some solace to know that (1) we're not the only one it happens to and (2) it's not the end of the road.

So, what does this have to do with your life? Think about a recent U-turn you've had to make or a detour you've had to take on the way toward *your* Montana—the life you're aiming for. What has that felt like? How have you responded? What has it taught you?

Now look back at a dream that has come true in your life. Perhaps that dream was paying off student debt. If so, was getting where you wanted to be (in this case, debt-free) an easy, straight shot without any disrupted plans or shattered dreams? Or did it take longer than you thought? Or did you pay the debt off quickly but had to make a lot of sacrifices in your social and personal life to make it happen? Did you run into any unexpected challenges or setbacks along the way?

The journey to the life we long to create often takes longer than we'd like, doesn't it?

You know, maybe that old cliché has some truth to it: "Life is about the journey, not the destination." Maybe the secret to contentment isn't found when we get something we want easily and on the first try. Instead, maybe contentment grows in all the hard moments that break us down—even when we feel stuck in a nightmare loop—as we learn to persevere each day.

Faith Versus Logic

Back in Lake Geneva, I took a deep breath as the sun glimmered off the water and slowly fell beneath the horizon. I reflected on the past week and looked ahead to the unknown future with a pit in my stomach. The breeze tugged at the stray hairs that had slipped out of my ponytail.

"God, where are You?" I asked, heart wide open and yearning for an answer to all that didn't make sense in my life.

I'd love to tell you that I heard, *I'm right here* or *Don't worry. This isn't where your story ends* or *It will all be okay. I promise.*

Something—*anything*—that either encouraged me or made even a sliver of it make sense.

But I didn't hear that. I heard only the breeze and the cries of seagulls overhead.

Matt walked up behind me and slipped his arm around my waist. "You okay?"

"I'm not sure," I responded, wiping a tear from my face. "I feel like faith and logic are at war within me."

He suggested I explain what I meant as we walked to get some dinner. As we strolled hand in hand toward the nearest restaurant, I said, "Faith says to keep trusting and hoping. Logic laughs at her and says, 'Don't be such an idiot.'"

Maybe something in your life has made you rethink everything you thought you knew to be true too. Whether that's what you believed about God, about another person, or even about yourself, those things can end up under intense scrutiny as we wrestle with heartbreak or even simple unmet expectations.

When you feel betrayed, let down, or completely shattered, does it ever seem like faith and logic are at war within you? Like it'd be easier to just quit altogether?

It's so hard, isn't it? It's like everything *in* you wants to keep believing but everything *around* you or that has happened *to* you makes it seem risky and even foolish. Sometimes it feels impossible—or at the very least useless—to hold on to faith that God is still working when none of it makes sense. And it takes courage to keep dreaming when the circumstances that surround you make it seem as though your life is more like a nightmare loop than a dream come true.

I'll be honest. I don't have a simple answer for you. I'm not going to toss you a cliché quote or even a Bible verse in an effort to make the confusion and doubt go away. In that season of loss, I found that filling my head with more knowledge didn't help get my heart and head on the same page at all. In fact, I wondered whether it made the chasm between them feel even wider.

On the contrary, it was actually when I allowed myself to sit in the tension of my questions, be loved and supported, feel the emotions I was feeling, and ask God to meet me where I was that I began to reconcile the faith and logic that waged war within me. But that didn't happen all at once that night in a corner booth at a restaurant in Lake Geneva. It happened over several months as I reluctantly let God show me who He really is instead of who I wanted Him to be for me.

So, rather than trying to convince you of anything, I'm simply going to pass on what my husband said to me over a charcuterie board as I expressed the battle happening between my heart and head. He said, "I get that. I'm struggling with that too. But that's why we can't rely on logic alone. It will always dare us to give up faith just when that is all we have left and exactly what we need most."

Since that day, I've held these words close. I hope that if you're stuck in a nightmare loop or if logic is screaming at you to give up hope, you give yourself permission to hold on to faith anyway.

Because, at the end of the day, after we try to get answers and fix what seems broken, we will find that faith is truly all we have left—and what we need most.

7

Unexpected Gains from Unwanted Pain

A few nights after returning home from Lake Geneva, I awoke from a deep sleep with stabbing pains.

Gasping for breath after each sharp pain and holding my lower abdomen in an effort to minimize the intensity, I shook Matt awake. "Babe, wake up! Something's wrong!"

He flipped on the light.

"What's wrong?"

"I think I'm having contractions!" I said between breaths.

I'm going to try to avoid being graphic here while still giving you an overview of what went on that night. Shortly after those sharp pains came on, I began to hemorrhage. That was *not* supposed to happen, especially after the surgery. I was nearly two weeks post-op, which meant I should have been at the end of my recovery. Instead, just when I thought I was almost fully recovered, it seemed like I was getting worse.

Matt called my doctor's emergency line, and they recommended either that we go to the emergency room if things didn't ease up within the hour or that I try taking some pain medication and then come into their office for an exam first thing in the morning.

At that point, getting in a car, walking into a hospital, and sitting in a waiting room sounded wildly uncomfortable, so we opted to try the latter option.

I quickly gulped down some Advil with a glass of water as we prayed for the pain to stop.

Within an hour or two, the contractions began to slow down and I had more time to catch my breath between them.

Finally, by 5:00 a.m., after passing whatever must have been missed during the surgery, the pain had turned into a dull ache rather than stabbing pains, allowing me to rest a bit more comfortably. A few hours later, the pain had almost completely subsided, and we went straight to my doctor's office as soon as they opened.

She performed an ultrasound and exam and then explained what had happened, reassuring me that my body was doing what it needed to heal and that I'd be okay. She prescribed a medication to stop the bleeding, as well as an antibiotic and a stronger pain reliever, just in case I had any other discomfort over the next couple of days.

Although I was relieved that the worst of the physical reaction was probably over, the emotional weight of it all hit me as we drove home. I was struggling to accept that just as I thought we could start moving forward, my body sent me two weeks backward.

"This is so, so wrong," I said to Matt through my tears.

"I know," he said. "But I will say, I'm so thankful we didn't go to Montana. I can't imagine going through this way out there, without being home and close to your doctor. I'm glad we listened to your gut."

After the appointment, I spent the remainder of the day resting on the couch. As I lay there, questioning everything I'd ever believed, my phone screen lit up on the table next to me.

It was a text from a friend, Lexi, checking in to see how I was doing.

"Do you want the honest answer or the comfortable answer?" I asked.

"Honest always," her response read.

"All right. Well, honestly, I'm in a really, really low place," I typed back.

Then I sent her an audio message to fill her in on all that I'd just experienced, without sparing any of the graphic details that I've tried to spare you here.

"Wow, that's traumatic, J," she replied. "Ugh, the unholiest of labors."

The unholiest of labors. I couldn't think of a more accurate way to describe it. That is *exactly* what it was.

As I read her text, I thought about all that had happened the night before. I remembered in the middle of the unexpected, painful episode, I had thought, *This pain would be so worth it if there was a joyous reward on the other side, like there would be in a normal labor situation. But this is literally all for nothing. On the other side, when it finally stops, it's still just going to be grief. This is pointless pain.*

I suppose one could argue that physical healing was on

the other side of it and that my body was doing what it needed to after an incomplete D&C. However, in a moment like that, when both physical and emotional pain collide in such a difficult way, that's not how you see it. It feels like your whole world is falling apart. You feel broken, angry, and confused at why such a god-awful thing would happen to you.

You may be wondering why on earth I'm telling you this. It's awfully personal. Quite honestly, as much as I'm trying not to be too graphic, I can still hardly believe I'm putting *anything* about this raw experience in a book for others to read. It's vulnerable and scary to share. If we weren't friends before, we sure are now.

I'm sharing it because, in a physical and literal way, it seems to represent a nearly universal experience that I think we ought to address: most of us have our own versions of an unholy labor.

I define unholy labor as labor pains that don't have the expected reward at the end of the hard work and, at times, agonizing pain and effort.

Before we continue, I need to be clear: Loss isn't something that can be directly compared to just about any other experience, really. Matters of life and death don't equate with occasions where you work hard and things don't work out. So, please hear me say that's not what I'm trying to do here. I'm simply using my story to illustrate a certain kind of feeling that many people face, but I'm *not* directly comparing loss to something lighter, like not getting the job you wanted or worked for.

So, with that in mind, let's continue. Labor pains, as we often think about them, usually lead to a joyous reward, such as laboring for hours to hold a beautiful newborn baby. Or, as a totally different example, working hard for long hours in the hot sun taking care of a garden or field so that fruit will grow. Remember, I'm using labor as a metaphor to highlight that we're often told that when we pour our blood, sweat, and tears into something, we'll have a generous reward on the other side of that effort.

These are normal labor pains. Labor pains that are worth it in the end. Unholy labor *doesn't* result in the outcome you've been working toward, hoping for, or praying for. It's when you pour all the blood, sweat, and tears into something only to come up empty handed and possibly in a world of hurt or in a worse position than you were before.

Outside the specific experience of labor that accompanies birth, there are so many things we fight for and labor over for hours, days, months, or years. We're promised by seemingly every motivational message that if we just endure the process and pain along the way, we'll be rewarded on the other side. But what about when that's *not* the case?

I used to believe that was a foolproof principle, but now I look at my own experiences with broken dreams and view this very differently. And I'd be willing to bet you've walked through your own, possibly very different, form of unholy labor.

Maybe you've been trying for years to do everything right while working toward a dream—whether that's to become a music artist, a doctor, an athlete, or something else—only to find that no matter what you try, you're left feeling more heartbroken or disappointed than before. As you process what's just happened, you sit there thinking, *Seriously?*

Or maybe you've toiled for years trying to heal your marriage, which has run into brick wall after brick wall. Every time you're about to turn a corner, something sets you back. Maybe you've discovered that your spouse has lied to you, cheated on you, or not followed through on his word.

All that time and effort for no reward and, in fact, only heartbreak.

When things don't work out the way we hope and our best efforts are met with *more* pain, it's easy to become disheartened, disillusioned, or even depressed. I'm no psychologist or therapist, but I do know from personal experience that when I become disheartened, I also become discontent.

Why? Well, because, instead of experiencing any kind of reward for my effort and pain, it seems as though I experience only disappointment. Naturally, that doesn't make it feel very meaningful or worthwhile, right?

However, my very literal experience with the unholiest of labors taught me something when it comes to the more metaphorical ones: even when we don't get the reward we were expecting, sometimes there is an unexpected refining.

As horrible as that whole experience was, I'm going to dare to say that when I reflect on all that has happened since, I've noticed something profound. I've realized that the pain that seemed pointless in the moment wasn't for nothing. It was refining. The dictionary defines *refine* this way: "to remove impurities or unwanted elements" or "to improve (something) by making small changes, in particular make . . . more subtle and accurate."[1]

Painful as it can be, refining essentially means that disappointment about lighter things (such as missing out on a promotion) or suffering through heavier things (such as loss or grief) has the power to remove distractions from what matters most, clarify our direction, and build our character unlike anything else can.

In other words, sometimes unexpected gains can be born out of unwanted pain. To my surprise, I *have* seen some very unexpected gains born out of difficult experiences where my efforts felt completely pointless. They may not have been additions I asked for or wanted, but they are important nonetheless. I want to share several of these with you in the hope that they'll give you encouragement that your pain or efforts aren't worthless, even when it seems like the reward is nonexistent.

Unexpected Gain 1:
Empathy

I'd heard this prayer countless times before: "God, break my heart for what breaks Yours."

If I'm honest, when life was all hunky-dory, it didn't matter how much I prayed that prayer; I just couldn't enter into someone else's pain, anger, or frustration and empathize with that person the way I would have liked to be able to. I could feel sorry for someone or recognize that something was hard or sad, but I couldn't truly understand. I couldn't feel that person's pain *with* him or her. I was so busy, so caught up in my own world, that even if I wanted to support someone well, my heart often was unmoved.

However, after walking through broken dreams and some of my greatest heartbreaks, I found myself tearing up over a friend experiencing a simple letdown as well as intense pain. And even when something didn't bring me to tears, I leaned into their experience rather than pulling away from it. I had become more empathetic. Perhaps it's because I had learned firsthand what it felt like to have my own experiences minimized by someone who couldn't relate or understand. I realized how uncomfortable it is to be pitied rather than heard, seen, and genuinely supported. Over time I noticed that I listened to others, instead of dismissing them, more than I ever had before.

Oddly enough, sometimes our deepest sufferings as well as the lighter almost-but-not-quite experiences give us the gift of eyes to see, ears to listen, and hearts to love deeper in a world that constantly tells us to just keep moving, focus on our own lane, and hustle our pants off to win a race that doesn't actually exist. Contrary to popular belief, I think it's not approval or achievement that we're really after but connection. Connection is key to contentment, and it's born out of empathy and understanding. As hard and horrible as they may be, our unholy labors, painful hardships, and frustrating setbacks have a way of deepening our connection—giving us more of what we're really longing for in this world.

Unexpected Gain 2: Patience

You know how they say patience is a virtue? Yeah, well, that's not one that I was born with. Every time a hope or dream has almost but not quite worked out, I go through a cycle of shock, denial, frustration or anger, and then eventually acceptance of whatever has happened. When I step into the very real tension of the in-between and embrace it, I become more patient, even if it feels as if I were forced to get there. I become more patient with my timelines and expectations, with others around me, and with myself.

I believe part of the reason that disrupted or delayed dreams are so difficult for us is that they screw up our timelines. And for naturally impatient spirits like mine, that is an absolute catastrophe. So much so that my first inclination when something goes awry is to rush to fix or replace it as quickly as possible.

Have you ever tried so hard to make something work that you spent more time hustling and striving than you did resting and persevering? I have.

As you already know, I'm no master gardener, but ask any good gardener and they'll tell you the importance of good soil and tending to your plants' growth. If the soil is in poor shape or isn't well tended, the plants won't grow to their full potential. Or consider farmers. The age-old wisdom was that farmers should regularly let their fields rest. In fact, in the Old Testament, the Lord instituted those times of rest for fields.[2] If farmers don't let their soil rest (or at least rotate crops), the soil—and therefore the produce quality—will suffer.

So it goes for us. If we liken our lives to a garden, this principle applies to us too.

If we don't take the time to tend to our bodies' and souls' needs so that they can be restored, we might find that, in spite of our best efforts, we end up in the same cycle of hustling for results that feel out of reach, only to burn out.

After my literal unholy labor, my body was tired. My heart was broken and drained. And my mind was so overwhelmed that I was experiencing severe adrenal fatigue and borderline depression. So as much as I *wanted* to try to make the crappy feelings and waiting (I told you I'm not patient) go away, I decided to pause.

I decided I would take some time to focus on slowing down rather than speeding up. In that time, I would try to establish sustainable rhythms and routines, investigate my health and what my body needed to heal, simplify and streamline my work schedule, go to therapy, and really invest in my marriage.

It was a tall order. But it wasn't a random list. It was an intentional list, and I gave myself the mission to set boundaries on productivity and create the necessary space to tend to these things instead of rushing to the next thing—even if the next thing was what I really wanted.

If you feel like no matter what you do, you just keep running into brick wall after brick wall, I invite you to give yourself permission to pause in your pursuit.

Pausing or slowing down doesn't mean giving up altogether and crawling into bed with copious amounts of Nutella as you hide from the hard or frustrating things life has thrown your way. You might need to do that for a minute or a day or two, and that's okay. But pausing isn't about staying in that place. It simply means taking a step back and looking at your garden or, in other words, your life. What needs tending? What is worn down or wilting?

And how can you slow down and clear some space to tend to those things?

Disappointments, suffering, and unholy labors have a way of inviting us to slow down like not much else can. When everything works out flawlessly or we reach a desired destination easily and quickly, we get what we want. However, when it doesn't go so smoothly, sometimes we get what we didn't even know we needed. While it doesn't feel good, it's in the fire that our character is refined. It's in those times that I notice a more patient, present, and intentional version of myself. And if you looked closely, I'd be willing to bet that the same is true for you.

Perhaps the unwelcomed, jarring nature of unholy labors—the ones that stop us in our tracks—present an unexpected invitation to *un-hurry our life.*

Unexpected Gain 3:
Clarity

That summer, I began to look at all my dreams and goals through a more critical lens, especially those I'd been pursuing professionally. It became glaringly obvious which goals were in alignment with where I truly wanted to go—and which were not.

As you'll read in more detail in the next chapter, sometimes adversity can lead to clarity we otherwise wouldn't have found (or even looked for in the first place). Adversity, including both everyday setbacks and life-altering kind of suffering, has always had a way of making me pause and reconsider what matters most to me. In a strange way, it removes distractions and helps me see more clearly.

Think about it. What adversity or unholy labor have you

experienced? What did that feel like, and how did you respond? And how, if at all, has it influenced your pursuit of your dreams as you move forward? Did it cause you to pivot? To set some things down and take a break? To reevaluate? Did it bring up fear of the future? It's important to acknowledge these things, especially if you're currently in a season of adversity. Although it may not always make the middle more pleasant, the clarity that can be born out of adversity often does help us see that it wasn't all pointless. Adversity can reveal the next right step in our journey.

Unexpected Gain 4: Discernment

After my experiences with unholy labors and broken dreams, I've realized that I've become more thoughtful about who I trust, what I do, and why I do it. I'm not sure why, but if I had to guess, I think it's because hardship—whether that looks like loss, tragedy, or being deceived—creates depth and discernment in a way few other things can. Perhaps it's only when you walk through experiences that shift your perspective—especially those that nearly break you—that you begin to weigh the risks of every decision, opportunity, and situation more than before. You may notice that you become much more careful in considering what's worth your time (and what isn't), which options align with your values, who you're willing to trust, and whose voices you'll listen to.

Life becomes less about impressing people or doing all the things and more about doing the right things—even if some people are unimpressed or don't get it. I guess, in a way, hardship has a way of shifting your focus from the unimportant and urgent to the ultimately important and eternal things. As a result, you become more thoughtful and discerning about every decision. In other words, you gain a better sense of what matters most to you, what you need to go toward, and why.

Unexpected Gain 5: Intentionality

After uncovering some health issues that I didn't know about before my losses, such as adrenal fatigue and an underactive thyroid, I had some decisions to make about how I would treat those issues and support my body going forward. One day, as I was driving to a doctor appointment and trying to decide whether to take a medication the doctor had suggested, I began to pray. *God, what should I do? Do I take the medication?*

I expected to get some sort of peace about whether to follow the treatment protocol she had recommended. Instead, all I got was *Love your husband well.*

That's it? That can't be what You're prescribing me. What does that have to do with medication?

The more I thought about it, the more I wondered if perhaps the decision to treat something medically was actually quite neutral and if perhaps the most healing thing for my journey forward would be to tend to my relationship with my husband.

As I drove, it dawned on me how easy it can be to allow a precious and sacred relationship like ours to be put on autopilot through chronic busyness (which we'd fallen victim to in the years prior) as well as grieving differently (which also applied to us). Unfortunately, it sometimes takes a massive disruption, devastation, or disappointment to help you see just how much you've drifted.

At least, that was the case for me.

With renewed determination to steward what I *did* have, I resolved to care for my marriage in ways I'd inadvertently neglected. A few weeks later, we sat down over dinner and I shared what I'd been reflecting on. Matt admitted that he'd been thinking something similar. So, right then and there, we made it our mission to outserve each other, especially when we're frustrated and tempted to do something to spite one another.

We began to implement that commitment in our everyday life, albeit imperfectly, and noticed a positive shift in our relationship. A few months later, I met with a mentor. As I shared all that I'd experienced recently and admitted how many sentences ended with question marks instead of confident periods, she listened, validated my experience, and then pointed out things I'd never thought of before.

She highlighted areas in my life, such as my marriage, that seemed to have received holy healing and redemption.

"That *is* a redemption story," she explained. "It may not have come how you expected or thought you'd have in this season, but this? This is worth celebrating."

From that conversation, I learned that redemption doesn't always come in the areas we think it will. Sometimes, through the breaking of one thing, something else that we didn't even realize needed healing is restored or strengthened. Sometimes unity and deeper connection with those we love—whether it's a spouse, friend, sibling, God, or ourselves—comes by way of the fire.

If you find yourself in the middle of unholy labor, even if not literally, I believe if you lean into it, right where you are, then one day—a month, a year, or three years from now—you will have the ability to say, "As hard as the path there has been, I'm thankful for how it has shaped me."

No Pain, No Gain

In all honesty, I would have preferred to never experience the letdowns and losses I did. I would have preferred not to "gain" any of these things. I would have been perfectly happy with my plans going off without a hitch and living in ignorant bliss.

As much as I wish that were the case and as much as I wish that unholy labors (literally and figuratively) never had to happen, I also try to acknowledge the power of the unexpected gains that can be born out of very unwanted pain.

Without such a jarring experience, I might never have slowed down, reconsidered what matters most to me, developed deeper empathy, and refocused on my priorities in the way that I have. That doesn't make terrible experiences good. It just means terrible experiences may not be as pointless as they seem.

Surprisingly, pain and suffering set me on a refining journey so that I wouldn't continue to take on too much, too fast, like I did in the first few years of my career. I slowly began to learn how to own my ambition without allowing my ambition to own me.

So, as hard as it is to say, perhaps success—true success—isn't always getting the outcome we labored and hoped for but instead is gaining the strength and refinement that come through disappointment as well as intense pain and suffering.

I wouldn't have believed it before, but today I can say that it's true: unexpected gains *can* be born out of unwanted pain. That doesn't make the crap any less crappy, and it doesn't make the pain any less painful. But it does give the unholy labors we experience some sort of meaning. Because although we'd prefer blissful ignorance and happiness, maybe God uses the unholiest of labors to create a holiness we otherwise wouldn't have had within us.

And maybe, just maybe, after some time, we can find a way to be thankful for the unexpected gains—the clarity, the growth, the character—that are born out of even the most unwelcome pain.

8

Adversity Can Create Clarity

Raise your hand if you ever feel *confused* about your dreams. Do you ever have a hard time discerning which dreams are truly yours, which just sound fun, and which are the result of pressure that society or someone else has put on you? I've been there. In fact, as you already know, I've been there to the degree that I closed down my very first company.

So, how do we get the clarity we need to walk in our calling?

I'm going to go out on a limb here and give you an honest but very unsexy answer: adversity. Yes, adversity. It may not be the only way to get the clarity you were looking for, but if my own experience with unmet expectations, disappointed dreams, letting go of good things, and even heartbreaking loss has taught me anything, it's that adversity can (and often does) lead to clarity.

The pain and problems we walk through often separate the wheat from the chaff. In other words, these experiences often reveal our direction while simultaneously unveiling distractions.

Here's what I mean: When something you've worked toward, waited on, or hoped for *almost* comes through but then doesn't work out, does it make you rethink everything? Maybe even doubt your dreams or reconsider what you're working toward altogether? This has certainly happened to me.

The more it happened, though, the more I began to wonder, *Is that really such a terrible thing? Could there be a gift in it?*

I've found that when I'm devastated by disappointment or feeling stuck—because I'm just short of reaching a dream or goal—rethinking everything can actually help me gain focus and clarity I didn't even realize I needed in order to succeed.

Experiencing the pain or frustration that comes with the disruption of a dream can help us reconsider all that we're pursuing. As we stretch ourselves like Elastigirl, trying to be and do all the things, the jolt of a heartbreak or a disappointment allows us to pause long enough to really think. To ask ourselves important questions that we otherwise might overlook because of our busyness.

Personally, some challenges, such as Matt's NFL career being cut short or closing down SoulScripts because I didn't know where to take it, created space to try new things I otherwise wouldn't have. With less on my plate, I had the space to clear my head and approach life and decisions more thoughtfully.

Additionally, deeply painful adversity—such as loss— eliminated nonessentials and distractions, and it forced me to slow down and reconsider everything I was pursuing, especially professionally. In the process, I began to see some things more clearly.

Setbacks into Setups

During my losses, I noticed that many people who reached out to express their condolences said something along the lines of "There are no words. I'm so sorry" or "I don't know what to say."

As I heard friends and family express that they wished they had the right words to provide comfort, it struck me. Words can be healing, but it's so hard to know the right things to say when hardship strikes.

Words have power. They can be either hurtful or healing, depending on how you use them. Unfortunately, so many of us just don't know what to say when plans go awry or hardship strikes. While we want to offer support or comfort, it often feels as though words fall short, or we may even say nothing at all because we're afraid to say the wrong thing.

So, after I recovered from my second loss, I began to seriously consider bringing back SoulScripts. As I thought about people often not knowing what to say and as I reflected on the roots of my shop, I realized that words have been my bread and butter all along and that SoulScripts is a *words* company.

For the first time, I saw a clear need that SoulScripts could meet. That's when the mission behind it became crystal clear: "We give you the words when you have none."

Whether those words provide comfort during a hard

time or encouragement toward a dream, words have the power to keep us moving when we get stuck. Perhaps this is why so many feel as though they don't have the right words to say. I shared this idea with a few friends, as well as with Matt, and everyone agreed: *This is it.*

So we made a plan to bring back SoulScripts in a meaningful, missional way.

I hired some additional help, and my newly built team agreed to relaunch it in October 2020, fourteen months after we closed.

In that meeting, I presented not only the need I wanted SoulScripts to meet but also the values, vision, and mission I wanted it to have. This wouldn't have been possible had the shop remained open the whole time. Well, perhaps it would have been *possible*, but it wouldn't have been as seamless of a transition. It's much easier to start fresh when something has paused than it is to try to change something people are used to interacting with in a particular way.

We announced the big news just a few weeks before opening the doors for a limited-edition collection, and the response was better than expected. Countless women sent in messages expressing their gratitude and excitement, many with selfies of themselves in the original product as well as stories of the impact the brand had had on them in the past.

On October 1 of that year, we held our grand reopening and were absolutely blown away by the response. In the following months, our sales outperformed what they had been before we closed, built at a more sustainable pace, *and* the company was able to operate with more direction and clarity. We received countless messages expressing how much the comeback and new collection blessed people—friends trying to support friends through sickness or loss, moms encouraging their daughters through hard seasons of life, women needing comfort or motivation for themselves in a season they felt stuck, and more.

After the initial comeback, we shifted from solely focusing on apparel to introducing resources, like journals, to help women navigate tough or simply mundane seasons with intentionality and from a position of purpose.

So, why do I share this story with you? Because when I closed the doors to SoulScripts, I thought I'd feel like a quitter or a failure for not being able to do it all. It wasn't until I stepped back from the middle of it—where it can be tough to see the forest for the trees—that I began to view it from a different perspective.

Oddly enough, what initially felt like a setback (closing the shop) turned out to be a beautiful and unexpected setup for this new clarity and direction that were born out of a season of adversity.

Perhaps the most eye-opening thing was the realization that I wouldn't have found this kind of direction and clarity had it not been for the adversity. While the clarity that came out of it didn't make the hardship itself any easier, it *did* help me see some of the purpose and meaning of it in a way I'm not sure I could have otherwise.

This is just one of many areas where I began to see what I needed to do (or not do) more clearly. You see, adversity has a way of making you audit your dreams when you otherwise might pursue things somewhat aimlessly. It offers you a new lens through which to see the things you do, the decisions you make, and the opportunities in front of you. In a unique way, it can clarify your calling—or an element of your calling—that once seemed blurry to you.

Gaining Clarity

If you feel stuck, unsure, or overwhelmed, I want to challenge you to consider your experiences with adversity. You don't have to have experienced tragedy or intense suffering either.

Just consider your journey—your own trials and triumphs. What have you walked through, learned, or overcome? Whether you're facing adversity right now or you've overcome an unexpected challenge in the past, start there, with those experiences.

Here's why: Those experiences give you compassion. They ground you in a mission bigger than just chasing ideas because they look or sound cool.

Then consider how those experiences might intersect with your skill set, experience, and/or education. Storytelling had become a skill of mine, and I would consider writing to be my craft. It got me started when I began SoulScripts as a tiny hand-lettering Etsy store that provided "encouraging words for the soul" back in my college days.

The experience I'd just lived, paired with the expertise I had developed over time, revealed an opportunity to serve people and fill a unique need in a way that would really fulfill me (instead of drain me). It wasn't until I stepped back, and even walked through some adversity, that I could see that clearly.

However, rather than putting out fluffy words, I was able to tailor how SoulScripts would use words to meet a need or solve a problem by leaning into my own story *even before* getting to the happy ending.

That gave it purpose it wouldn't have had if everything had come easy. In other words, I had the chance to lean into something that brought me joy and fulfillment in the middle—between where I started and where I expected I would be.

That special space is there for you too. Your experiences have set you up to do something unique, and stepping into that will be fulfilling (even in the middle seasons).

As you cultivate a life you like—one that brings you contentment, peace, and clarity, even before you get to where you want to be—consider how you can couple your experiences with your expertise to show up in this world with purpose and empathy.

Starting with the adversity we've faced can help us cut through all the pressure, noise, and options clamoring for our attention and instead see our unique opportunities—what it is that will bring us true joy and contentment—so much more clearly.

We may even find that whatever it is we're looking for is so much closer than we think and that, rather than building something that merely looks successful, we can choose to build something that is full of meaning.

So, if you're stuck, frustrated, and rethinking everything, please never forget these truths:

- Clarity is often found in adversity.
- Slowing down might help you find what you're looking for.
- Sometimes what looks like a setback can actually be a setup.

And, friend, your story—even in the middle of uncomfortable (and painful) *almost* seasons—really, really matters.

9

When Your Dreams Come True for Everyone Else but You

You know what makes it really hard to be content with your life? Feeling like your dreams are coming true for everyone but you. *Can I get an amen?*

It was late July, barely a month after our second loss, and we decided to go on a vacation with my family to Lake Tahoe. A few days into the trip, I sat on the edge of the pier with my toes dangling over the lake when my phone chimed. I picked it up to see a text from a colleague, telling me about a big win she'd just had in her business. Given that my professional aspirations and plans had been thrown off course multiple times that year by both personal and global crises, I could almost physically feel jealousy creep in. *How did she manage to do that? I can't seem to catch a break!*

I began to type a response, but I was struggling to find the right words. As I tried to make sense of why it seemed so easy for her—while I kept running into brick walls no matter what I had tried so far that year—I began to delete the words I had typed. The waves rolled in before me as I took a deep breath and decided to wait to respond.

Not long after that, my phone chimed again with a text from a friend sharing her big news: she was expecting.

A golf-ball-sized lump formed in my throat, and I nearly dropped the device in the water. I stared at the message for a moment in disbelief. *You've got to be kidding me. Why is she even telling me this? And how am I supposed to respond?*

I debated what to do.

If I tell her I'm happy for her, it'd feel like I'm lying because I don't feel happy for her right now. But I can't tell her the truth, can I? That would be rude.

Have you ever found yourself in situations like these? You know what I'm talking about, right? Those moments when the very things you've been hoping, working, and praying for seem to work out seamlessly for everyone else?

Just days after your heart gets broken, your best friend gets engaged. Hours after your kid gets into big trouble, your neighbor posts about their kid's big accomplishment on Facebook. Or just weeks after you get turned down for your dream job, your sister gets a huge promotion.

It's like getting throat punched just when you thought you were getting back up.

Someone tells you their big news, and you freeze as all the thoughts rattle through your brain.

Ouch! This is so unfair.

I don't feel happy about this.

But I know I'm supposed to be happy for you.

It would be rude not to respond.

How do I respond, though?

SOS.

Again, I decided it might be best not to respond in the moment. My emotions were high, and I didn't want to take away from her joy simply because I couldn't share it. So I set my phone down, looked out over the water for a moment, and then walked into our Airbnb to get a Popsicle as I sorted through my thoughts.

As I thought about everything, envy crept back in. Then guilt for feeling jealous. Of course, that only made the problem worse.

So I texted my therapist to get her input. After explaining the situation, I said, "I'm having such a hard time being happy for others and feel like a terrible friend."

First she validated my feelings, and then she sent a follow-up response: "Being happy for others is a social norm, but it's often not how the brain actually works in situations like this. Take some space, and give yourself however much time you need."

Being happy for others is a social norm but not how the brain actually works.

She went on to explain that there are a lot of misconceptions around being happy for someone. We often assume that to be happy for or celebrate someone, we must feel the same elated feelings that person does. That's not always as easy as it sounds. Instead, we can show our support without necessarily feeling overjoyed or throwing a big party for them. In other words, it's possible to be supportive while still feeling sad, confused, or discouraged ourselves. Supportiveness and sadness can exist simultaneously, and sometimes, to authentically support those we love, we need to take a step back first.

All I'd ever thought was that the *only* appropriate response was to match someone's happiness with the same level of excitement. Perhaps it's the expected thing to do, but I wanted to find the most *genuine* and *healthy* thing to do.

Plus, as a Christian, I was familiar with the verse that says, "Rejoice with those who rejoice; mourn with those who mourn."[1]

Except I wasn't sure what the appropriate response was when you're mourning the very thing someone else is rejoicing over. Are you supposed to jump up and down with that person, even if that feels disingenuous? Is there a way to support a friend's joy without ignoring or denying the very real feelings that their joy may bring up for you?

I wonder whether operating with this principle—that we can acknowledge our hurt instead of responding to someone with fake happiness—might have saved so many of us from years of built-up resentment or hidden jealousy by actually giving us permission to validate our feelings and take the space we need to be able to support them *genuinely*.

Over text, that may look like waiting a bit to respond so we can gather our thoughts or even vent our feelings to someone we trust. In person, that may look like offering congratulations but then taking the space or time we need to process the sting after the encounter.

Perhaps for the first time in my adult life, I gave myself permission to not pretend to feel happier than I was just because that's the perceived expectation. I would take a little time to work through the initial blow so that eventually I could genuinely support my friends, even if from afar.

As I sat on a lounge chair outside the Airbnb with my Popsicle in hand, my brother happened to walk around the corner. "Hey," he said. "Why so blue?"

"Aw, hey, buddy. Just a little bummed out today."

"Well, what would make you *not* so bummed out?"

I shrugged. "I don't know. Maybe buying a big inner tube somewhere, floating out on the lake, and unplugging for the rest of the day."

A huge grin flashed across his face. "Let's do it!"

So we loaded into the pickup truck and headed down to the local hardware and grocery stores to see whether either of them had inflatable rafts or inner tubes. Negative on both. We tried another store, and it didn't have any left either.

"Wow, who knew inflatable rafts would be *so* popular around here?" I joked as we left and looked out at the massive lake across the street.

In a last-ditch effort, we stopped by one more store. To our surprise, it *did* have inflatable rafts, although they weren't exactly what I was thinking.

"Well, Jord," he asked, "do you want the flamingo or the unicorn?"

I thought for a minute. *Definitely* the flamingo.

The clerk was kind enough to inflate it for us, and I spent the rest of the afternoon floating on a big pink flamingo in the sun, sipping on a cold drink.

As weak as my faith felt at the time, I talked to God a bit too. I admitted the bitterness I felt as I compared myself to my friends. I asked for help to believe that even when it didn't make sense, He was writing a beautiful and purposeful story not only for other people but also for me.

Did it take away my pain or disappointment? No.

Did it make the situation feel any fairer? Not at all.

But do you want to know what it *did* do?

It helped me remember the bigger picture when it seemed like everything in the world was unfair and when I began to believe the lie that everyone else's dreams but mine would come true.

The lesson here? You don't have to pretend that an unfair or triggering situation doesn't bother you. Sometimes the best thing we can do is to pause, collect ourselves, breathe, and trust that the middle we find ourselves in isn't the end of our story.

As the sun set that night, I typed a response to both of my friends along these lines: "Huge congratulations to you, friend. What an exciting time for you. I want to be honest in saying that this is a difficult season for me, and I don't want to project any negative feelings in a season that should be one of so much celebration for you. Please know I'm loving and supporting you from afar."

I added a couple of heart emojis, hit Send, and held my breath as three little bubbles appeared to let me know they were typing a response.

Guess what happened?

No one was offended or upset. In fact, they both responded with understanding and even gratitude for my authentic response!

How about that?

In situations like these, I think we often believe we need

to force a feeling we're *supposed* to have, even if that feels ungenuine in the moment.

That day I learned that when we're met with the sting of seeing our dreams come true for someone else, it *is* possible to honor a friend's joy *and* be honest about our feelings without making that person feel guilty for the good that is happening in their life. When you're stuck in the middle and it seems like everyone around you is on to the next milestone, give yourself some grace and, when possible, space. Float on a big pink flamingo if you have to. As difficult as seeing your dreams come true for other people can be, try to look at it as *more* than a reminder of what is painful. Instead, dare to believe it's also a reminder of what is possible.

The Other Side of the Comparison Trap

A few weeks later, one August afternoon, I was sitting on my back patio, sipping lemonade and attempting to tan my thighs, when a peculiar thought came to mind.

I've spent so much time over the last month comparing myself to others and feeling behind, I thought. *But I wonder whether women have looked at my life and compared themselves to me and felt behind in other ways.*

I thought about my single friends who often shared that they wished they could find a decent guy. How did they feel on my beautiful wedding day? I wondered whether they felt a little like I did in that moment, comparing myself with women who had something I wanted but didn't yet have.

I thought about my friends who felt unfulfilled in their careers. I realized they had probably compared their careers to mine at one point or another, even when I ran into obstacles in my business. Surely it was tough for these friends whenever I'd share about challenges I was having in my dream job, right?

I grabbed my phone and texted a few friends to ask them about this so they could either confirm or disprove my hypothesis.

To my surprise, it was confirmed. One had, in fact, found herself feeling behind in the whole marriage department compared to me, and another had certainly looked at her career and felt like she'd accomplished nothing in her life compared to me.

Wow, I thought, *we're all doing the same thing, just in different ways.*

No one is behind; we're all just in different places. For example, many friends who have never experienced loss and easily had several kids haven't experienced the fulfillment I have from my career. Some other friends who are flying through career milestones haven't found the right partner or have had their hearts shattered by the person they thought they'd be with forever.

Just as I felt behind in one area of life, women all around me felt behind in another area.

Putting things into perspective this way taught me something I want to pass on to you. Keep this in your back pocket when you look around and feel as if your dream is coming true for everyone but you: We all will struggle in this life. It may be at different times and in different ways, but we were never promised easy or perfect lives, although society and social media tend to shout, "You can have it all," causing us to think having it all will make us complete.

The truth is, we may not be able to have it all at the same time. There may be a season when we have the family we hope for but can't yet afford the dream house or can't move as fast toward our professional aspirations as we'd like. Or there may be a season when we can quickly advance in our careers but don't have the dreamboat husband or cute kiddos yet. It all comes in phases, friend. And those phases look a little different for each of us.

Before I go on, I want to address what you might be thinking. You might be thinking about someone you know personally or follow online. She's got the nice house, the doting husband, the darling kiddos, the looks, the successful career. She sure seems to have it all. I suppose it depends on how you define "all." Is it possible that she has a chronic health condition that you can't see? An estranged relationship with her mother? Childhood trauma that affects her daily? Of course it's possible. In fact, it's likely that there is something that disrupts her life daily—even if it appears picture perfect to you.

However, just in case you're really certain she does have it all, let's say her life is as perfect and painless as it appears right now. Sure, it may be possible to seemingly have it all for a little while. I'd call that a good season—a gift to cherish and enjoy because it won't last a lifetime. It probably won't even last long. I can almost guarantee that some part of it will inevitably get disrupted. Whether the company makes staffing changes, a global pandemic hits, or someone in the family gets sick or goes astray, it won't stay flawless forever. Something will almost always get disrupted for every single one of us, just as it seems like all the pieces are falling into place. Why? Because we live in a fallen world and life is messy. I wish I had a better answer for you, but I'm not sure that's something we will ever fully understand on this side of heaven.

So, instead of trying to decide who has it better or worse or wondering whether we're behind, perhaps it's important to remember that everyone's almost-not-quites look a little different and everybody's season of suffering and/or waiting comes at a different time. Some experience it during childhood, others experience it in their twenties, and some don't come face to face with disrupted dreams or broken hearts until later in their lives.

But the bottom line is that we all will face it at some point or another; no one is immune. Not even the woman who you think has a picture-perfect life. Just like I've experienced, that sense of having it all and having it all together can shatter in the blink of an eye.

Comparing your existence with others' experiences only robs you of your own contentment. It inhibits your own processing and journey toward your ambitions—your aim in life. Focusing so heavily on what is happening in someone else's life also keeps you from seeing the way God is working in yours.

When your "perfect" plan faces a painful obstacle, you can focus on the obstacle and compare your life to the lives of those who don't have the same hurdle to face. Or you can focus on your life and celebrate how far you've come despite said obstacle.

Of course, the question becomes, "Cute sentiment and all, but how do I actually do that? Especially when it feels like everything is going wrong in my world?"

Move in the Meantime

When life feels utterly unfair, jealousy sprouts. Jealousy leads to bitterness. Unchecked, it's like a weed that chokes our growth. Rather than flourishing where we are, we begin to feel strangled by and stuck in our circumstances. Naturally, we peek over and see how wonderful someone else's existence seems to be, how effortlessly that person seems to be flourishing, and before we know it, bitterness makes us believe the lie that we're behind. As a result, we get stuck. Sometimes we get so stuck that we don't even recognize opportunities or open doors in front of us—because we're so focused on the one that got shut.

Since that day at Lake Tahoe, I've had to consistently push myself to remember that a life of contentment and purpose isn't about being ahead or finishing first. Instead, it's about *choosing* to flourish even when we feel behind or don't have it all (because that will be most of the time), hold on to faith, and believe the truth that someone else's success in a particular area isn't our failure.

I know—this sounds nice in theory but feels impossible to put into practice. Quite honestly, I haven't figured out how to just reprogram my feelings on the spot. I'd imagine you haven't either. It's not as simple as saying, "Never mind. I don't feel that way anymore." This is why choosing to flourish is more than merely deciding to feel differently. It's taking action. It's changing our focus and allowing our feelings to follow suit. For example, when we begin to feel jealous, behind, or discontent, choosing to do something that feels enjoyable and life giving—such as making our favorite dessert, reading a book on the back porch, volunteering for a cause, or planning a fun double date—can help shift our focus from *I'm behind* to *Even here, I will find ways to like my life.*

In other words, when unmet expectations and broken dreams leave us feeling like we've fallen behind, how we tend the ground we're planted in can make a big difference.

When I mope around and tell myself I'm stuck in some way, I begin to believe the lie that I'm running out of time. Focusing on how far away I am from a personal or professional milestone I expected to be at creates a pretty miserable feeling. However, when I shift my gaze away from my expected timeline and focus my energy on creating a lovely life (gardening, volunteering, journaling, cooking, floating on a lake, etc.), I experience the sense of satisfaction that I'm looking for and that I believe I'll find when I finally get to that milestone.

I admit that I don't always get this right. Sometimes I get stuck in a funk and do the very opposite of what I know I need to do. I admit that because I'm sure that despite your best efforts, the same thing may happen to you. That said, I can physically feel the difference it makes when I do. I feel lighter, more alive, and fulfilled. If your circumstances have left you feeling behind, I want this for you too.

When I begin to feel stuck or behind, three questions help me make the choice to tend to my life:

1. Compared to who?
2. What desire is unmet in my life right now?
3. How can I care for the desires of my heart even before a dream comes true?

Let's unpack each of these.

1.
Compared to Who?

Who am I comparing myself to, and how can I consider the bigger picture? As I shared before, when I zoom out from the one area or issue I'm fixated on, I find that the person or people I'm comparing myself to likely feel stuck or behind in a different area.

Whenever you begin to believe the lie that you're somehow behind, consider who you're comparing yourself to. Then zoom out. Look at the *whole* picture, not just the specific area where you feel behind, and you might just realize that what you're believing isn't based on the whole truth.

2.
What Desire Is Unmet in My Life Right Now?

When you trip just short of the finish line or fall short of a goal—or everyone else's dreams besides your own are coming true—I want you to consider something. Instead of fix-ating on the specific thing you wish were happening, try to concentrate on the deeper desire underneath it. If your dream is to get married, then your deeper desire is likely love and companionship. If your dream is to reach the next level in your career, then your deeper desire may be to create or achieve. If your dream is to grow your family, your deeper desire may be to nurture.

The list could go on, but I'm sure you get the point. When you begin to feel behind, stuck, or discontent in your almost-but-not-quite achieved hopes and dreams, consider the deeper desire that feels left out to dry when one specific dream shatters or takes longer than you'd like. This is critical to understand for step 3.

3.
How Can I Care for the Desires of My Heart Even Before a Dream Comes True?

Although those desires may not be met in the way we'd like or in the timeline we'd prefer (things like finding a spouse, having a family, or building a fulfilling career unfortunately aren't as simple as picking something off the Target shelf), we *can* find ways to tend to those good desires before we get to where we want to be and while we wait on a specific dream.

Will it be the same as it would be if our dream came true? Of course not. Still, I've found there's something powerful in moving in the meantime (rather than moping around and comparing myself with everyone else).

For example, a few months after my second loss, I felt a

deep, unmet need to nurture. It was like an empty feeling, and that was really hard. After a while, I began to ask, *What can I nurture right now?* I chose to pour into my health and marriage, as well as start a garden.

That garden was the one I shared about in chapter 1—the one that I planted late in the season and that failed miserably in terms of the physical harvest. But it met a deep need for me in that season. Although it wasn't at all the way I originally planned to nurture, it was an enriching way to move in the meantime.

The details may be different for you. Let's say that something has come up in your personal life and thrown a wrench into your plans to build a career as a music artist. Your desire to create through your music has been put on hold. Does that mean you can't still create? Not at all. What you create in this season may just look different than you thought. And you may be able to fulfill that good desire by volunteering to work at a summer music camp for underprivileged children, leading worship at your church's Sunday gatherings, or doing something else that is still aligned with that dream and feels fulfilling. Plus, you may be surprised to see how doing so could hone your vision, refine your talent, and shape your future—for the better.

When it seems like your dream is coming true for everyone but you, the goal isn't to pretend that everything is fine and dandy. The goal is to have an action plan to recover from the gut punches and shake off the lie that you're behind. Doing so allows you to be present, grounded, and content in the sacred place you've been assigned to grow today.

Remember, just because you may not be at your destination doesn't mean you're at a dead end. You're simply on divine middle ground. I dare you to find enriching ways to move even here, in the middle, even as you feel stuck between where you started and where you hope to be.

10

Uproot the Lies You Believe

When something goes wrong in your life, do you ever catch yourself looking to the left and right, noticing that everyone around you seems to have it easier? And then do you think, *Ugh, why me? Why is this happening to me?* If you could see me right now, you'd see me sheepishly raising my hand.

I'm sure you've asked that question too. When someone else gets picked for the third job promotion in a row, maybe you've wondered, *Why?*

Or when you discover that an employee has been stealing from you, you might look at your best friend's seemingly perfect business and wonder, *Why is this happening to me?*

Maybe you had a tough upbringing and feel like you're always one step behind your peers. When the days are long or you see someone else seeming to advance in life as if it's a total breeze, you might look at your background and wonder, *Why me?*

If you have an illness or injury and everyone else in your

community or age demographic appears to be healthy, you might be tempted to ask, *Why me?*

If you've experienced a loss that few of your peers can truly understand, you might also ask that question.

I'm sure that if you have a heart beating in your chest—if you're human—you've asked some version of the *Why me?* question at some point or another.

While I believe it's only natural to ponder this question when we feel behind, hurt, or discouraged, I also know how stuck it can make us. If we're not careful, we might begin to dwell on it, which leads to a downward spiral. Then it becomes even more difficult to get back up, hold on to hope, and keep showing up for what matters most.

Why *Not* Me?

One evening, my friend Mel came over to catch up. She brought dinner and a bottle of wine to share, and we sat at my kitchen table, talking for hours. After she caught me up on her life a little bit, she looked me in the eye, put her hand on my arm, and asked, "So, how are you doing?"

Mel's not someone I can lie to. I thought about the losses I was still grieving, as well as several other ways I had felt let down in the last year. I told her that I'd been asking *Why me?* a lot more than I ever had in the past.

I said, "It just doesn't make sense. I know I'll probably never know the answers, but I want to know why these things have happened to me. Why have so many things felt upside down and painful? Every time I thought I was going to catch a break, it seemed like something else went sideways."

Mel thought about my question for a minute before responding. "I know I haven't had all of the same experiences as you," she said, then took a bite of her pasta. "But I have asked questions like that too. In fact, I ask myself that question a lot when it comes to singleness. So often I would look around at happy couples and think, *What am I doing wrong? Why isn't this happening for me?*"

Phew. At least she doesn't think I'm crazy.

She continued, "But God never said life would be fair or easy for any of us. And as much as I wish hard things wouldn't have happened to you, a part of me also kind of wonders, *Well, why* not *you, J?* Is it possible that the very things God has allowed you to go through will be part of what He will do through you? What if these experiences are what will shape you to step into what He literally created you to do?"

Unsure what she meant, I gave her a skeptical look and asked her to go on as I scooped another serving of buttery pasta onto my plate.

"I just don't think any of it is meaningless," she said. "I hate that you had to experience so much heartache, but I can't help but believe these parts of your story will be used to create such positive change in the world. So, as sucky as it is, why *not* you? Why not me? God can—and does—bring beautiful things out of our setbacks, struggles, and even suffering. And I believe the things you've faced are just the beginning of something beautiful."

In the moment, I couldn't decide if I was encouraged or annoyed by those words. In all honesty, I didn't want to be shaped or refined. I wanted to be happy, whole, and comfortable. I wanted things to work out. *Why not just snap His fingers and make me ready for whatever He had for me?* I didn't want to walk through frustrating setbacks, and I didn't like the idea that a good God would need to use struggles and suffering to prepare me for something—even if it *was* part of my calling. But then Mel and I talked about Jesus and how even He walked through the blazing fire of suffering to fulfill His destiny—for the benefit of you and me. Immediately I saw it differently. I saw that the ways of God, while difficult to understand or fully comprehend, may not need to make sense to me in order to hold some kind of uniquely divine beauty.

As we wrapped up our conversation, I hugged her neck and thanked her for her encouragement. We cleaned up the dishes as we chatted a little longer before she left.

As I've already shared, unexpected gains can be born out of unwanted pain. So, why do I bring this up now? I share this conversation with you because it jolted me when my friend flipped the question on its head and asked, "Why *not* you?"

Although it took a little convincing, that conversation ultimately encouraged me in all the right ways.

It's important to note that Mel said this several months after some of the blows I'd experienced, which is why I was able to receive it. Had she said this the day after one of my losses or in the middle of what felt like absolute chaos in my business as we pivoted at the start of a pandemic, it wouldn't have been received the same way. I wouldn't have appreciated a perspective like that, even if there was truth to it.

So, if you're reeling from a recent blow, whether that's a deeply painful loss or simply inconvenient chaos, those words might not resonate with you in this moment. And that's okay. Right now they don't have to. Sometimes it's not until after we have time to process and start to move forward that we can receive encouragement like this. Otherwise, it doesn't always feel like encouragement.

A few hours later, I crawled into bed and opened a book I'd been reading, *A Grace Disguised* by Jerry Sittser. I devoured several chapters until I came to a spot that stopped me in my tracks. Chapter 9 was titled "Why *Not* Me?"

I had to read it again just to make sure my brain wasn't playing tricks on me. Clear as day, the title still read, "Why *Not* Me?"

No way.

I dove right in. The chapter essentially focused on how life isn't fair—much like Mel and I had talked about hours earlier—and the author shared about wrestling with the question *Why me?* when he walked through grief of his own.

It was well past midnight, but I read on, soaking in every word. These paragraphs affirmed everything Mel had said:

> I once heard someone ask the opposite question, "Why *not* me?" It was not a fatalistic question because he is not a fatalistic person. He asked it after his wife died of cancer. . . . He could no more explain why his life had turned bad than he could explain why his life had been so good up

to that point. Did he choose to grow up in a stable family? Did he have control over where he was born, when he was born, or to whom he was born? Did he determine his height, weight, intelligence, and appearance? Was he a better person than some baby born to a poor family in Bangladesh? He concluded that much of life seems just to happen; it is beyond our control. . . .

"Why me?" seems to be the wrong question to ask. "Why not me?" is closer to the mark, once we consider how most people live. . . .

Can I expect to live an entire lifetime free of disappointment and suffering? Free of loss and pain? The very expectation strikes me as not only unrealistic but also arrogant.[1]

I set the book down as I tried to catch my breath and digest those deep words. Perhaps I was asking the wrong question all along. Maybe Mel was right. Maybe I needed to start asking, *Why* not *me?*

When we operate from a place of *I deserve XYZ* or *It should be easy,* whether we're focused on something simple or something more serious, we're lacking an important perspective. I know that's hard to hear, but if we look around at all that we've been unexplainably blessed with while considering how so many suffer, we might be slower to get stuck in a victim mentality.

It's a humbling experience, to say the least. When I think about Jerry's words in light of my own experiences, it makes me think, *Why shouldn't hard things happen to me? They happen to everyone—and I'm no better than them.*

That doesn't make what's missing hurt any less, nor

should it invalidate very real feelings when life shakes us to the core. It does, however, offer perspective so that we can learn to look through a lens that helps us zoom out from our narrow view of the world and see reality more fully. If you find yourself asking, *Why me?* I want to encourage you to flip the script and start asking, *Why* not *me?*

I think we sometimes need a reality check on the subtle expectation that difficult or disappointing things happen only to others. As Sittser pointed out, that's a pretty inaccurate, and perhaps even arrogant, thing to think. We all will have crosses to carry. In a world that says we should want to have it all, God is in the business of transforming us into the strong, world-changing women He created us to be, even if that's through hard things.

We have an opportunity to embrace our setbacks, struggles, and sufferings—not to run from them but to let Him use them for good. To be honest, sometimes I can't help but wonder whether the pain we trudge through and disappointments we face could be the birthplace of more than just dreams. In fact, perhaps it's in *those* places that we uncover and are prepared for our calling—how we will cultivate lives that aren't just easy but that truly leave a legacy.

Uproot the Lies

Besides the "why me?" question that is rooted in the misbelief that we should be immune to hard or seemingly unfair things, other unhealthy attitudes and tendencies can spring up when life knocks us down or disrupts our dreams.

Someone once told me, "Be careful how you talk to yourself, and be mindful of the thoughts you entertain. It only takes two hundred thoughts to create a belief."

In other words, if I think *This will never work out for me* two hundred times, that thought solidifies as a belief in my heart.

She explained that once something becomes a belief, it's much harder to remove because it grows roots. It becomes like a monster weed in a garden and takes a lot of work to uproot.

Have you ever let the lies of comparison or a victim mentality take root in your life—maybe through thoughts like these: *This will never work out the way I hope* or *It's just not going to happen for me*? If you're honest and answered yes, you're in good company here. I've been guilty of this very thing.

Do you want to know what helped me? Ripping out weeds.

I don't say that as a cute metaphor. I mean it literally.

Allow me to explain. It was a late summer weekend, and Matt and I realized we needed to catch up on some yard work we had neglected all season. Our poor property had begun to look abandoned. So we started with the planting beds. For whatever reason, the original owners of our old house thought it was a good idea to put a thousand massive planting beds all over the three-acre property. Okay, maybe it wasn't a thousand, but it sure felt like a thousand. Of course, they were a pain to maintain, and we hadn't had much time to take care of them.

Many of the weeds had grown as tall as me, so I put on some gardening gloves and got to work. At first, they came out of the ground with just a little tug, but then I found some real beasts that had developed roots like those of a small tree. It seemed like no matter how hard I pulled, they just refused to budge.

As I pulled with all my might, lighting up every muscle in my body, I decided to do something I'd never done before. I would assign each weed a lie that I'd been believing and that had begun to take root in me.

"This weed, this massive one, is the lie that my body betrayed me," I said to no one but myself as I thought about the losses I'd experienced and used every fiber of my being to give it one last big tug.

Fueled by determination to get that dang lie ripped out, I kept pulling until the roots of the weed began to tear. I pulled just a little harder, and the roots tore away from the soil so quickly that I almost fell on my backside as it came out of the ground.

I couldn't believe it! I had gotten it out! With my Air-Pods blasting music in my ears, I threw a mini dance party to celebrate the accomplishment. I looked down the driveway to see Matt in his backward ball cap shaking his head and laughing at me.

When I came across another seemingly impossible weed, I did the same thing.

"This is the lie that God has forgotten about me."

"This is the lie that I'm a failure."

"This is the lie that XYZ not working out is all my fault."

"This is the lie that my business projects will always fall short of my goals."

"This is the lie that my dreams are doomed to end in disappointment."

So on and so forth.

Every time I assigned a lie to a weed, I somehow found the strength to get it out.

Some were a real fight, but the significance of what I was doing gave me the grit and determination not to give up until I got every single one uprooted.

By the time the sun began to set, my back ached and sweat covered my shirt.

Matt walked over after he finished mowing the lawn. "Wow, someone's been working hard!"

I laughed and responded, "Who knew that pulling monster weeds could be so empowering?"

For the first time in months, I felt that I had my strength back. I didn't feel like a weak and hopeless woman overcome by despair or entangled in the lies I'd been believing. I felt that I had some say over what I'd allow to take root in my life . . . and what I absolutely would not. All because I had decided to face the lies head on and rip them up unapologetically, even if it nearly broke my back.

I want you to do something similar. Consider some of the lies you've been believing as a result of your own broken heart, unmet expectations, or disrupted dreams. Maybe, like I did, you think God has forgotten you. Maybe you think your hopes or dreams will just never work out. Maybe you think it's all your fault that some things have gone wrong. Maybe you believe you're unworthy. Maybe you think it will always be like this.

Call out all the toxic thoughts like that. And then assign

them to a physical activity. It doesn't have to be pulling weeds, although that's probably the most accurate illustration of the work you're doing in your heart. If it's winter or if you're blessed not to have weeds, consider other ways to do this. Perhaps you can clean out your closet and get rid of old items you don't need but have been holding on to for one reason or another. For each item you get rid of, assign a lie to it as you put it in the trash or donation bag.

It doesn't matter exactly what you do; just do *something* that allows you to acknowledge the lies you've been believing and take action to let go of things that can represent what has taken root in or cluttered up your heart.

Does it totally get rid of the thoughts? Not necessarily, but it certainly helps you make progress. And there's something healing and empowering about that.

Plant in Faith; Root in Love

Not too long after my weed-pulling endeavor, Matt and I decided to plant our very first garden. You know, the one that didn't exactly yield a harvest. It was late in the season, early August, but I didn't care. I thought having a garden might be a healing project for me—it would give me something I could nurture.

However, I quickly learned that tending a garden—especially when you don't naturally have a green thumb—is hard and holy work. *Stewardship* is hard and holy work.

Grocery stores and Amazon Prime give you what you want the second you want it. Gardens are different. Plenty of factors affect your harvest (weather, insects, etc.), and it takes *time* before vegetables come up.

Interestingly, though, not getting every outcome you want makes you appreciate what you *do* get. That first year, I was so darn proud of those few kale leaves that grew, especially because the carrots and other plants didn't work out so well. If anything, that one kale plant showed me what could be possible if I made just a few adjustments.

While the first attempt wasn't a great success, I was fulfilled and challenged by the process. I decided I'd get better with practice and tried again the following season. The second time we tried our hand at gardening, this time in a new home (more on that in the next chapter), I caught myself thinking about the fresh start that a new home—with new ground—represents. For a reason unbeknownst to me, the words *plant in faith; root in love* played on repeat in my mind as I placed the starter plants and seeds in the soil.

I thought about what those words might mean.

Plant in faith. To plant is to make an investment with the faith that your garden will bear fruit at just the right time. Maybe that's what God was asking me to do with my dreams. To show up, prepare the soil, plant in faith, hope in what was unseen, steward before I could see anything, and then trust that fruit would come at just the right time.

Root in love. As I stood there in my old overalls with the sun beating down, planting new life in the hope that it would take root, it dawned on me. We fight the lies that we believe not only by pulling them out but also by rooting ourselves in love.

Bible verses I had studied years earlier came to mind:

I pray that you, being rooted and established in love, may have power, together with all the Lord's holy people, to grasp how wide and long and high and deep is the love of Christ, and to know this love that surpasses knowledge—that you may be filled to the measure of all the fullness of God.[2]

Rooted and established in love. Filled to the measure of all the fullness of God.

Somehow, in that sacred moment in the dirt, I realized that, in all my dreaming, perhaps I'm really longing for something even deeper. In all my toil and striving, desiring, and achieving, I'm longing for Eden.

Or, at least, what Eden ultimately represents: heaven, a garden of life, wholeness—the fullness of God.

In this place, this life between two gardens—the Garden of Eden and eternity with God—I could reach every milestone, achieve every dream, and crush every goal and *still* feel incomplete if I'm not rooted in Love. And love isn't just a feeling. It's not just a choice. It's Someone. It's God. Because God is Love.

The wholeness we're looking for as we reach for our greatest dreams was once found in the Garden of Eden and is ultimately only found in unity with God.

Perhaps that's why, when we get something we thought we wanted—the new car, the spouse, the promotion—it feels as if the finish line moves. In other words, the satisfaction we thought we'd feel isn't there (at least not for long). We just long for the next thing, always feeling *almost* where we want to be. Maybe it's because we were never made to be fulfilled by even the greatest things this world has to offer.

We were made for God. We were made for the garden. Interestingly enough, according to the creation story in Genesis, the first job God gave humans was to tend the Garden of Eden—to steward it. I believe He's given both you and me a similar calling. Whether you have a green thumb or not is beside the point. Our deepest desires will be filled by God alone. And our job is to tend to our lives—and those in them—with care and intention at *every* stage of our journey, not just the ones where we reap a reward.

As I reflected on the significance of this, I began to uncover the truth that I mentioned at the beginning of this book: *This life isn't a game to win. It's a garden to tend.*

Never mind the messages that say having it all will make us happy. We know the truth: that dang finish line is always going to move just when we think we've almost made it. There is no having it all outside the fullness of God.

With that in mind, how do we overcome the lies that discourage us so we can keep showing up for what matters most when we're faced with disrupted, delayed, or even seemingly destroyed dreams?

We acknowledge and validate the pain we're experiencing.

We identify the lies that have taken root in our lives.

We rip out those lies with reckless abandon.

We brush the dirt off, stand up, and get moving again.

We plant our dreams in faith and root ourselves in Love.

And we tend to the lives we've been given, right here.

We make the most of the in-between because our entire lives on this earth are lived in the middle—between two gardens: the Garden of Eden and eternity with God in heaven.

Because if our dreams are truly God-given and part of our legacy, we can't mess them up. We're just not powerful enough. In fact, nothing is powerful enough to mess up His plan for our lives. As we tend to the life in front of us and take steps toward what's next for us, we must anticipate pain and disappointment so we can find the strength and determination—the ambition—to grow in the middle of the unknowns and almosts.

Growth toward what matters most and contentment in spite of—not outside of—challenges are what a successful and fulfilled life is made of.

11

Prioritize Your Priority

Matt and I strolled up our long driveway while returning from our daily walk on a crisp September morning. I looked up at my old colonial farmhouse, then glanced around at the property it sat on.

"What's on your mind?" Matt asked.

"I was just thinking how much this place reminds me of myself," I responded. "It has so much potential, but wow, it needs a heck of a lot of work."

He laughed. "That's one way to put it."

We'd already done several renovations and invested a lot of sweat equity in the landscaping. This led to a conversation about whether we wanted to continue doing all the work that was required to maintain and upgrade the place. With an older house on a three-acre property, something always needed to be taken care of. It seemed like every time we finished one repair or project, another two or three would pop up.

As we chatted, we began to recognize how stressful it was to manage a property like that while also building businesses and eventually having a family. One young couple can do only so much!

When we bought it two years prior, we were newlyweds and thought it sounded fun to have our own small-town version of *Fixer Upper*. HGTV makes home makeovers look so much easier and more fun than they are. Updating an older home seemed like a cool project for us to do together—that is, until we had to live and work in that home while it was constantly under construction.

It was fun for a bit, but the fun didn't last long. We eventually got so busy traveling that we were rarely home long enough to keep up with anything around the house. The costs of the renovations we'd tackled were adding up, mice were mysteriously sneaking in every other week, and the constant half-done state of the place made it difficult for home to feel like a refuge. Then we suffered both losses in that home. With all the memories filling the place, I began to itch for a fresh start, a change of scenery, and a simpler lifestyle. You know, one that didn't require a kitchen remodel, an expensive repair every other month, or maintaining three acres of yard.

Although we've always been interested in homesteading and certainly have it on our list of long-term dreams, the initial reason we were so drawn to the house was somewhat arbitrary: it had Instagrammable potential, and we saw what DIYers did on TV. So naturally, we wanted to try it too.

As we navigated the work and expenses of upkeep and as the newness of renovation projects wore off, having an

HGTV lifestyle wasn't so appealing anymore. In fact, it became overwhelming—a seemingly never-ending burden on our time, our energy, and our wallets. We began to see the truth tucked into Ecclesiastes 3:1: "There is . . . a season for every activity."

Perhaps a homestead and HGTV home makeovers would be part of our future. But given all the ups, downs, and almosts we'd just experienced, we began to reevaluate whether it was a priority for us in *that* season.

For weeks we went back and forth about whether we wanted to sell or continue doing remodels. We had made so much progress on the house, from renovating two bathrooms to updating a living room to simplifying the landscape, it seemed like it was so much closer to where we wanted it to be. With the progress we had made, the thought of stopping before all the projects were done felt like quitting early. Unfortunately, though, the remaining projects—a new roof and windows, kitchen remodel, and exterior paint job—were the most time intensive and expensive of them all.

As we discussed options, we challenged ourselves to ask questions like "Do we *really* want this?" and "What is our top priority: renovating an old farmhouse or removing unnecessary stress to focus on our health and family?"

Then we asked, "Does living in this home support our priority in this season, as a young married couple, or is this a source of stress that could be taking away from this priority?"

Although we didn't want to admit it, we both knew the answer: the latter. We knew we could renovate an old farmhouse in the future if we so desired but we couldn't get back these years of our youth. Sometimes it takes losing something precious to show us what truly belongs on our plates and what doesn't.

Still, even knowing the right answer, choosing to move forward with selling was one of the hardest decisions I had to make up to that point in my life. I wasn't just letting go of a house; I felt as though I were giving up on the vision I had for the home and the dream it represented for our family.

I had planned to paint the house white, replace the windows and shutters, put a new roof on it, and knock out walls and remodel the kitchen, which was tucked into a corner with virtually zero counter space and yellow cabinets, circa 1980 colonial style (*not* cute).

I had imagined we'd have our babies there too. I had decided which room would be the nursery, and I thought I'd see my children crawling and frolicking in the backyard under the big sycamore as we restored the old home to make it our own.

But it was becoming a money pit. We barely had time or resources to get to some of the bigger projects we wanted to do because as soon as we'd start to make a plan, the second-story shower would start leaking through the floor (and into the kitchen ceiling), or the furnace would go out, and we'd have to write a big check to get that repaired (or invest hours trying to repair it ourselves). It was almost always one step forward and two steps back, and that was beginning to feel absolutely unnecessary.

Regardless, parting with the house meant releasing the vision I had for it, and that caused me to go back and forth on the decision for over a month. On the one hand, I knew I'd feel relieved if I were to just let it go. On the other hand, I didn't want to let it go too soon only to regret it later.

It's not as if the home were being taken from me against my will. Instead, I would be voluntarily walking away from it and releasing my expectations for what I thought would come of it. It felt backward.

I wonder if you can relate to this. Can you think of a time when the original vision you had for something—a home, a career, or something else—no longer suited your needs or your family's needs?

If so, you know how it is. *Even* when you're sure it's absolutely the right thing to do, it can feel nearly impossible to pull the trigger and follow through.

I must have discussed the decision with everyone I knew and analyzed it from every possible angle. I asked every what-if question in the book. We even put the For Sale sign up in our yard for two days, and just as our realtor was about to officially put the house on the market online, I called him and told him I wasn't ready!

We pulled the sign down so I could mull it over just a little longer and drive my poor husband crazy in the process. *Oops. Sorry, babe.*

I share all this to make a point that has shaped me and my dreams: Recognizing our priorities is one thing. Recognizing our top priority—singular—and *acting accordingly* is another thing entirely. That requires releasing our expectations and taking real action, usually painfully difficult action, as we focus on the primary thing we're aiming for.

Why is this important? Because if you lack a clear and

meaningful priority, you might end up being pulled in different directions and torn between what you thought you wanted and what you truly need. Trust me—that is a frustrating place to be.

Less Is More

Do you ever feel overcommitted or overwhelmed by what you're doing, even if it started off as a good thing? If you answered yes, have you ever thought about why you feel the way you do or, in other words, why you may have bitten off more than you can chew?

We tend to overcommit ourselves when we're unclear on what we truly want (the priority), why we want it (the purpose), and how we're going to steward it (the pursuit).

To clarify, when I talk about what we truly want, I don't mean materialistic desires like a fancy beach house or luxury car. I don't mean arbitrary goals that sound impressive. It's deeper than that. I'm talking about knowing the priority in this season of your life in a world that tells you that you should somehow manage to balance everything—in a world that dares you to think *everything* should be a priority.

Having a clear priority doesn't mean you do only one thing with your time. It means all that you do should somehow *support* the priority, not take away from it.

In fact, did you know that the word *priority* didn't always mean what it does today?

In the book *Essentialism*, Greg McKeown explained, "The word *priority* came into the English language in the 1400s. It was singular. It meant the very first or prior thing."[1]

He went on to say that it was singular for about five hundred years and then we tried to turn it into a plural:

> Only in the 1900s did we pluralize the term and start talking about *priorities*. Illogically, we reasoned that by changing the word we could bend reality. Somehow we would now be able to have multiple "first" things. People and companies routinely try to do just that. One leader told me of his experience in a company that talked of "Pri-1, Pri-2, Pri-3, Pri-4, and Pri-5." This gave the impression of many things being the priority but actually meant nothing was.[2]

That last line hit me hard the first time I read it.

This gave the impression of many things being the priority but actually meant nothing was.

Let that one sink in.

Do you know what this means? It means that when we say we have "priorities," we actually don't hold *anything* as a true priority.

This doesn't mean that multiple things aren't important—they absolutely are. Your health, your work, and your family are all incredibly important things to steward. How could you ever pick which gets to be *the* top priority?

It's not exactly as simple as focusing 100 percent of our time and attention on one and forgetting the rest. So, what do we do?

We reframe how we think about our priorities or, more appropriately, our *priority*.

Rather than considering all the important things in my life to be top priorities, I've found it helpful to consider the *present priority*, or, as I like to call it, the PP. This is the main priority to focus on in a particular season. Each important aspect of my life can then serve a unifying purpose and should move me closer to that present priority.

Allow me to explain how this can look by illustrating how it played a part in our difficult decision to forgo the vision we had for our colonial farmhouse and simplify our lifestyle.

Now, I certainly didn't expect to be uprooting my life and starting over just two years after settling down. I *expected* to be turning that house into our dream home and raising our first baby under that roof. That's what I *wanted* to be doing. But since life didn't exactly go that way, I had to consider the next best steps to take with our present priority in mind.

As we looked at all that was on our plates, we identified a present priority: our health. Why? For the sake of our family. Our health—emotional, mental, spiritual, and physical—had taken quite a hit over the course of the year prior with all the travel, stressful home projects, double-shot espressos, and late nights of work. Investing in our well-being and managing stress felt like the right focus for that season.

That meant all that affected our health, including work and other stressors, needed to be tended to in a way that would support the PP.

In other words, with my present priority clearly in mind, all decisions I made regarding important aspects of my life (work, house, social activities, etc.) had to be aligned with that priority.

We did a full audit of our lives to identify unnecessary

stressors, as well as issues that needed to be addressed with intention, so we could ensure that all we were doing supported our health rather than taking away from it.

The house was an unnecessary obligation in that season and was more of a stressor and distraction, so the house needed to go. We reasoned that simplifying our house burden would open up time and resources to invest in our health and restore ourselves (instead of pouring all our energy into restoring an old house). So as October drew to a close, we finally decided to move forward with putting our house on the market.

Similarly, unnecessary stressors I identified in work were either minimized or delegated. While work was certainly important, I began to shift the way I approached it so that it would fall in line with the priority. I could no longer be run by achievement and excessive productivity and expect to also prioritize my health for the sake of our family. I had to take the necessary steps to ensure that I owned my ambition rather than allowing it to take over what I knew was most important to me.

Notice the difference. Although these areas of my life are incredibly important, the actions I began to take in those areas were centered on a common priority. I rearranged the way I approached these things so that the pursuit of the priority would be more sustainable. As my commitments fell in line behind a clear priority, they became easier to steward because I no longer approached them as individual priorities to somehow hold in perfect balance.

All the commitments and lifestyle changes I made in

that season pivoted around the priority itself, including the decision to sell the house.

Define Your Priority; Act Accordingly

When disrupted plans or unmet expectations force you to rethink your dreams and ambitions, try to see that as an opportunity—even a good thing. Instead of getting stuck in the chaos, zoom out from all the noise, distractions, and "priorities" you're trying to balance. Then allow the disappointment or even heartbreak to be an invitation to reevaluate your life and rearrange it around what you decide matters most.

Take the following steps to prioritize and move forward.

1.
Identify the Present Priority

What do you truly value? What is your priority in *this* season? Silence all the voices vying for your attention and telling you what to focus on or do. Be still. Consider what matters most to you (or you and your family). Try to focus on a single priority so that you have a clear aim.

Ask, *What comes first? Is there something that is time sensitive and that needs more care and attention than other commitments?* For example, Matt and I decided that what we needed to focus on most in that season was our health as an investment in our future family. From taking steps to support my mental health and getting plugged into a church to rebuild the foundation of our spiritual health, to seeking answers and restoring my body through nutrition and lifestyle, these things desperately needed time and attention.

If your present priority is to pay off all consumer debt, your lifestyle decisions and daily commitments should fall in line with this priority. You should ensure that the investments you make and resources you use support it in the best ways possible. Your professional and social decisions should fall in line with that as well. You might pick up odd jobs or freelance on the side to bring in extra income, or when you join your colleagues for a drink after work, you might choose to order a lemonade instead of the twenty-four-dollar fancy martini.

Allow yourself to have a priority (such as stewarding your health) rooted in a clear purpose (such as for the sake of your family or future family)—a focus that guides your decisions in this season of your life. Not only will this make you a better steward; it will also help you pursue the right goals for you, overcome the pressure to keep up with others, and embrace the tension between where you are and where you hope to be.

Even when you face a heartbreak or setback, making sure that all facets of your life support your priority can help you move forward in the right direction.

Take some time to consider *your* present priority, and be sure to be clear and specific. What do you want all the important areas of your life to move you toward? This will allow you to bring your "priorities" under the direction of a single true priority.

Remember, it's the priority for *this* season. It may change down the road, so focus on the short term—the weeks, months, or even a year in front of you. Define a possible priority for this time of your life, and then move on to step 2.

2.
Consider the Purpose

Consider the present priority you chose. Before finalizing that as the priority and rearranging your other responsibilities accordingly, ensure that you can answer this question: *Why* is this the priority?

As we discussed the possibility of making our health the present priority, we asked ourselves, "Why is it important to make this the PP?"

The answer was easy: for the sake of our family. You might not think that selling a home has much to do with stewarding your health or that prioritizing your health has much to do with your family, but they have everything to do with each other.

Here's why: I learned the hard way how much stress can affect my health. In fact, when I began health testing after my losses, I found out I had severe adrenal fatigue, likely from years of chronic stress and busyness, and I knew it was time to change some things. There's no way around the fact that my health is important to our family. To be clear, this doesn't apply only to pregnancy. Whether or not you're in your childbearing years or wish to have children at all, I believe this is still true for you. Our health directly affects our family and others we interact with. If we're exhausted, hormonally imbalanced, or feeling miserable, that can have a direct impact on our marriage, children, or other close relationships.

I wanted to take some time to simplify our life, reduce mind clutter, and tend to our well-being so that we could be in a healthier place as a couple and as individuals.

I'm sure your situation looks a little different. Perhaps your priority in the present is to pay off student loans and save up money (the PP) so that you can go on a yearlong mission trip next year (the purpose).

Remember, this is about *your* life and the purpose driving what you do and the goals you pursue. This is not about instant gratification or fleeting things like an arbitrary weight or financial goal. This is about establishing a big-picture vision that can keep you committed to the priority that you pursue. Your *why* may be to share the gospel in unreached areas, have a family of your own, become debt-free, change the health-care system, or something else entirely.

This big vision is a tool to guide you; it's the foundation for your present priority and gives you a reason to ensure that your time, effort, and resources support it. Allow this purpose to ground the things that you do, the dreams you pursue, and the present priority you choose. When you find yourself overwhelmed, stretched too thin, or disappointed when things don't go according to plan, ask yourself, *Why am I doing what I'm doing? Is what I'm doing still aligned with my* why? *How does this support that purpose—or doesn't it?*

3.

Make an Action Plan

Once Matt and I defined that particular season's priority of improving our health, rooted in a clear why—our marriage and family—I began to consider how everything else would fall in line accordingly. This is where those other important responsibilities that we generally refer to as "priorities" come into play.

Rather than considering my home and my work two different priorities, I began to ask, *How can what I do with my house or with my business best support* the *present priority?*

This brings these two seemingly very different responsibilities into unity, working with each other, rather than pulling me in different directions and working against each other.

The decision we made to sell our house is a great example of the priority in action. Once we identified our health as the present priority and, therefore, determined that trying to live an HGTV lifestyle was not, it became clear that it was time to simplify. As that became clear, I realized I could invest the funds and time I would have spent remodeling and repairing an old home into our health and healing instead. I could put some of the funds I would have spent on an expensive new kitchen into savings, as well as pursue testing and work with doctors to improve my overall health—all while limiting stress by living in a home that didn't require endless repairs.

Do you see how this works? When we identify the priority, important areas of life begin to have more unity as we act in accordance with that priority.

I want you to explore what this may look like in your life, especially if you're in a season of heartbreak, disappointment, or unmet expectations that have made you rethink everything. Once you've defined your *why,* as well as the present priority that aligns with it, consider the areas of life that require the most attention or time from you. What steps do you need to take to bring each one of the important facets of your life into alignment with the present priority?

Evaluate each aspect of your life—including your professional goals and obligations, your home and its needs, your health routines, your relationships and social commitments, and your finances. As you look at each one, ask, *Why? Why am I doing this? Does it support the priority?*

If yes, leave it. If no, move on to step 4.

4.

Remove Distractions

If something on your plate doesn't support your PP, ask a follow-up question: *Can I adjust how I'm doing this so that it better supports the priority?*

If the answer is still no, try to find a way to minimize it or remove it from your plate entirely (this is how we came to the conclusion about the house). Limit or remove those commitments that distract or take away from what matters most to *you*—not what you think others want or expect you to do.

In creating your action plan, it's critical to consider roadblocks or distractions that may throw you off course or hinder your progress. Once you know what you're aiming for in the bigger picture, as well as the priority to focus on now, it becomes easier to identify what you definitely don't want or need to be doing.

Like I said, it became evident that completing home renovations was more distracting than it was supportive of the present priority. So we made the decision to move.

When we began to pack, I found that we had boxes and boxes of stuff that I'd collected over the first few years of our marriage. I spent a lot of time going through what I wanted to hold on to and what I was unnecessarily allowing to take up space. As I took bag after bag to the local donation center, I felt lighter. By quite literally lightening my load, I realized I could do the same thing in many other areas of life. What nonessentials was I carrying around in my mind and heart or keeping on my schedule?

Simplification became the name of the game as I tried to steward the priority.

Your job now is to ensure that you minimize anything that can take away or distract from your present priority. What might need to be changed or completely thrown out to accommodate the priority you've defined?

Listen. I know how hard it is when your perfectly laid plans face an unwelcome interruption. I know the pain and frustration that come with loss or unmet expectations. I sit here in a home I didn't plan to be in. A year ago, I thought I'd be standing in my little farmhouse's updated kitchen with a baby on my hip. Instead, just when my vision *almost* worked out, I ended up being thrust into a journey I didn't sign up for. The journey often has me feeling as though I'm hiking through a valley miles from where I thought I'd be in life by now. It hasn't exactly been fun or easy, but it has been refining. And as I consider the peace a simpler life has brought me and peek out my office window and see the homes of treasured new friends across the street, it reinforces that although it's not what I expected, God has a plan for me and right now I'm exactly where I need to be.

So, my encouragement to you is this: Don't allow disappointment or a painful disruption of your plan to be a dead end. Allow it to be your invitation to a new beginning. You might not uproot your entire life and move, or you might. Regardless of how much or how little you change, please remember that rethinking everything isn't always a bad thing.

Sometimes? Sometimes it's the very thing we need to truly succeed.

12

Make the Most of the Almosts

After a few years of marriage, the last thing I expected was to move back in with my parents. When we sold our house, we realized there would be a two- to three-month gap between when we had to be out of our old house and when our new house would be ready.

Only a handful of months prior, I *thought* I'd be ending the year enjoying a newly renovated kitchen with my cute little family. And it *almost* worked out that way—until it didn't. Instead, just before Thanksgiving, we found ourselves moving our furniture into a temporary storage unit and unloading suitcases in my parents' basement. I couldn't help but think how opposite this was from my expectations of how that year was *supposed* to end.

As I reflected on the year that had just passed, so much felt upside down.

Then, as I looked ahead to the upcoming year—a vast canvas of unknowns and question marks—I desperately wanted to fill it with something, anything, that would make it make sense. The way I had imagined the year (and the rest of my life) going was drastically different from the reality I was living. And I wasn't sure what to do with myself.

What do you do with the unexpected white space in your schedule, the empty bedroom in your house, the place in your heart that something special—a lover, a child, a friend, a position—was *supposed* to fill but now cannot? When you feel stuck in limbo, straddling the tension between where you are and where you thought you'd be? I tend to busy myself. I try to fill the space or the silence with a jam-packed schedule and distract my mind from what feels out of place—even if what feels out of place is myself.

I shared these thoughts with my friend Jenna, and she said, "You don't have to fill the in-between space with busyness, though. You can steward it. I truly believe this is your boot camp in learning how to be more present and still."

This is your boot camp in learning how to be more present and still.

I thought about what she said for hours. Her words dared me to believe it was possible to shift my perspective and see this painful in-between as preparation for the life I wanted to lead. Rather quickly, I shifted from feeling empty to feeling empowered.

This season of my life can be seen as one of two things, I thought. *It can be something I try to avoid and distract myself from, or it can be something I lean into, embrace, and make the most of. I can avoid it through busyness and distractions, or I can steward it with careful intention.*

As I began to think about what a boot camp could look like, I decided to tend to some important things that I'd neglected for years while I was so busy achieving.

Although I had said my health was my present priority, at first, I wasn't entirely sure what tending to that would look like outside of eliminating stress. So I took time to research, test, and ask questions. In the process, I learned how to manage my blood sugar, eat whole foods, cook meals I love, cut back on caffeine, and regulate my sleep patterns. In just a few months, I noticed a drastic difference in how I felt. I began to have more energy, strength, and focus than I'd had in years! I used to rely on coffee for that. Now I rarely drink coffee at all.

I focused on my mental and spiritual health too. I started journaling, got involved in a church community again (something I'd avoided for quite some time), mentored some younger women, and volunteered to serve others. After wallowing for a while, I decided I didn't like how any open moment would turn into an opportunity to obsess over what I didn't yet have or what I didn't like about my life. Pouring into and showing up for others gave me perspective and a sense of purpose I'd been missing. Oddly enough, getting outside our own heads and lives to serve can come with plenty of unexpected blessings. These may include an overwhelming sense of gratitude for what we *do* have, the joy that comes as a by-product of blessing someone else, and more.

When the space I'd carved out to renovate my dream house, publish a book, and raise a baby was disrupted, delayed, or left empty—when I felt like my life wasn't going anywhere but was instead stuck in pending mode—I began to see that maybe it was a season God would use to grow *me*.

If you find yourself with unexpected emptiness, straddling the tension between where you are and where you expected to be (or believe you're supposed to be), I want to invite you into your own boot camp.

A boot camp, in its original context, is designed to prepare someone for combat. While you may not be going off to an actual war, I believe this word is so appropriate for a couple of reasons.

First, whether or not we can see it, there *is* a war going on—a war for our minds and souls. That war has been raging since the fall of humanity at the beginning. When we're dealing with the questions and frustrations that come with pain and unmet expectations, the battle gets even more intense. It's as if logic and faith are at war within us. Faith says to keep trusting. Logic—or perhaps really the devil—laughs and says, "Don't be such an idiot."

It's easy to want to forget God altogether when we feel as though He's let us down or flipped our plans inside out for no apparent reason. I know because I did. I pushed Him away because I felt betrayed. This is the battle you and I face every day—especially when life doesn't go our way. The more prepared we are, the more we think on what is true, noble, right, pure, lovely, and admirable—as a verse in the book of Philippians tells us to do[1]—the more we will be prepared to fight the good fight of faith when the devil tries to use discouragement, disillusionment, and discontentment to sow seeds of doubt.

Second, I wholeheartedly believe the almost-but-not-quite moments that catapult us into a valley of questioning ultimately prepare us for something. And not just anything—something great. In the wilderness, we can meander or we can walk forward intentionally. For months I kind of wandered aimlessly. I think that's only human, especially when our plans or even our entire sense of normalcy has been shaken to the core. But there's a point at which we have to decide whether we want the between places to ruin us or refine us. We can focus solely on the problems the wilderness brings, or we can allow it to prepare us for a bigger purpose—even if that purpose is one we can't yet see.

If I learned anything during my own boot camp season, it's this: the pain of the valley isn't a punishment; it's a privilege. It's a training ground to prepare us for our calling. It's in the tension that our character is refined. It's there that we gain the tender strength, empathy, wisdom, and perseverance that we need to succeed at what truly matters in this life.

However, it's important to remember that a boot camp like this should be *more* than a means to an end. It's not simply about crossing a finish line only to look up to heaven like, *Hey, God, I'm ready for my prize now!* (Although it would be nice if it were that easy).

In other words, don't view it as something to just hold you over or keep you busy until you get to where you want to be. I hope that if you, too, tend to live at breakneck speed, this will be the first step into a more lasting lifestyle change. You know, to give your mind, body, and soul the support they need to be able to sustain your God-given dreams (whatever those may be).

Your boot camp may look different from mine, but if you're feeling stuck in an in-between season like this, here are a handful of ideas of what you can be doing to make the most of this time.

Focus on the Things You Need to Do

I don't know about you, but there are a lot of things I *want* to do.

I *want* to have clear skin for good. Today I *need* to eat a well-rounded lunch to manage my blood sugar and keep my hormones balanced.

I *want* to have a successful career. Today I *need* to do the unglamorous thing and write a few thousand words with focus and intention.

I *want* to have an incredible marriage. Today I *need* to make the small decision to put my phone down and connect with my husband over dinner.

The same is true for you. Every day when you get up, challenge yourself to focus on the small things you need to do in the present instead of obsessing over what you want to have in the future. Why? Because every move you make today shapes who you become and prepares you for what lies ahead.

We spend so much time looking to the hopes we have for the future or entertaining the fears we have about it that we can easily fail to do what we need to right now to prepare for what's coming. I'm on a mission to change that in my life one meal, one meeting, and one moment at a time.

Whether you want to study the Amazon rain forest, become a world-famous painter, have a family of your own, or get healthier, identify what it is you want to do. What are you aiming for? Then ask yourself, *What do I need to do today, right where I am, to move me just 1 percent closer to that?*

And do it.

Create Sustainable Rhythms and Routines

Have you ever watched a video or read a blog post by an influencer sharing her picture-perfect morning routine and felt overwhelmed by all that she does before 7:00 a.m.? I'm raising my hand because I have.

Sometimes I see that type of post and wonder, *Really? Do you really get up before 6:00 a.m., then work out, walk the dog, make your bed, read for an hour, prepare your lunch, do a face mask, shower, get ready with a full face of makeup and super-model hair all in the first hour you're awake?*

I mean, hey, if that works for you, great. But I'm sorry—I tried all that once. It lasted a week. I just couldn't maintain— nor did I like—all the to-dos before my day even started.

So I decided to do what works for me. I would commit to consistently doing only one or two things every morning before starting my day. In my boot camp season, those two things were (1) going for a walk and (2) making my bed.

Of course, I also did the basic things like brushing my teeth and putting on real clothes. But I wanted to have just one or two (not ten) additional disciplines that would allow me to start the day with intention.

I considered morning walks my quiet time to pray or just

reflect. I do a lot of sitting at a computer during the day as it is. Walking, instead of sitting and reading, allows me to clear my head and heart, prepare for the day, pray, and experience the fullness of God. This created something I could consistently look forward to, and it helped me start my day from a place of connection, contentment, and peace (rather than chaos).

If you're experiencing a season of waiting, healing from heartbreak, or just trudging through a disappointing time, remember to see this as a boot camp. Sometimes implementing a simple routine that will get you out of bed each morning and allow you to connect with God can make a big difference.

Consider what would work best for you and how you could add some *simple* routines and rhythms like this to your life.

Learn Something You Didn't Know Before

Did you know that, on average, deer live only about three years in the wild? What about the fact that we have an endocrine system? Ever heard of that? I hadn't. Have you ever learned how to play a mean game of poker? Know much about how taxes work? How tomatoes grow?

These are just a handful of things I learned—during my boot camp season.

I didn't know much about wildlife, had absolutely no idea how my own body worked, never understood why people liked to play poker, and clearly struggled to keep plants alive. That is, until I decided to get curious. I decided I wanted to learn about nature and spent more time listening to my husband, a passionate hunter, when he rattled off all the fun facts about deer. I started reading more books too. I read books on topics like finances and women's health. I asked my dad to teach me how to play poker, and although I'm no gambler, he took me to a local casino to play video poker so I could learn the hands. I got the hang of it and won a hundred dollars. Hurrah!

I could rattle off a dozen interesting things I've learned about how the world works, but I'll spare you and instead just encourage you to take time to learn. When you're in a season of waiting, facing an almost-but-not-quite experience, or stuck between where you started and where you hope to be, dare to discover new things. Read a book you normally wouldn't. Ask more questions. Explore somewhere you've never been before. Watch a documentary. Get curious. Just because you're a grown-up doesn't mean you have to stop exploring and asking questions. Let yourself walk through this life with the wonder you had as a child. You might be surprised by what you find—you might uncover fascinating new knowledge or find a skill or hobby you really, really like.

Serve Others

Careful not to overextend myself only to burn out, I began to try to say yes to more than just focusing on myself—my wants, my needs, or my achievements. Each quarter, I tried to focus on one or two ways I could do something special for someone else. I started small. For example, one month, Matt and I considered which causes we could donate to. A couple of months later, I reached out to some younger women I used to mentor and invited them over to talk and reconnect. I had taken some time to refill my own cup by meeting with mentors of my own first. Pouring into those young gals was more life giving than I originally thought it would be. A few months later, I hosted two bridal showers for women I love. The following quarter, I reached out to the community director at our church and asked about volunteer work Matt and I could get involved in. For years we'd been saying we wanted to open our home to those in need. After kicking around the idea for months and after settling into our new home, I knew it was time to finally walk the walk. We applied for a program with a local nonprofit and took the first steps toward opening our hearts and home in new ways.

I share these examples with you because I want you to see that you don't have to fly across the world to serve someone else. Whether you open the doors of your home to celebrate someone's big milestone (graduation, marriage, or something else), extend your hand to the needy in your community, or just show up for a friend who needs someone to listen, serving others comes in many shapes and sizes. It doesn't matter what you do or how you do it. Just understand that when our own lives feel hard or when our goals seem to get stuck in *pending*, sometimes the most sanctifying thing we can do is step outside ourselves and show up for someone else. Don't be afraid to put yourself out there *before* your life is everything you want it to be—especially when everything in you says it'd be safer to isolate and shut down.

Simplify

As we moved into our new home, I unpacked only essential items and left most of the stuff I wasn't sure what to do with—the decor items, books, and other things that didn't quite have a place yet—in boxes that we stored in our basement. Very quickly I discovered that I functioned better with less. Clear surfaces, open space on my walls, and cozy touches to warm up a room—such as a bit of texture in our light fixtures or a simple throw blanket—served us better.

It makes sense, really. My friend Myquillyn Smith pointed out in her book *Cozy Minimalist Home* that "scientific research has shown that the level of cortisol—a stress-response hormone—rises in women when we are faced with the excess stuff in our homes." It's been proved that clutter causes us to feel anxiety and stress. Apparently, it's not as common in men as it is in women.[2] *Lucky us.*

In addition to unpacking only the essentials and items that cozied up a room without cluttering it, I created some systems for our new place. For example, I put a basket on our counter to catch all the clutter that would otherwise end up all over the island (wallets, sunglasses, keys, etc.).

This makes it easy to keep surfaces clear, as my husband isn't quite as much of a neat freak as me and prefers organization not to be too complicated. Clear surfaces, I've found, keep me feeling calm and happy. And that's good for both of us.

On my mission to reduce stress and focus on my spiritual, emotional, and physical well-being, minimizing clutter in my daily living spaces has been so rewarding.

That said, physical clutter isn't the only thing that can cause stress. Mind clutter—or an excess of stuff to do—in our work and our personal lives can have a similar effect.

I knew that certain projects I had committed to were distractions—just more things on my plate—adding stress to my life rather than supporting my priority.

When I began to choose *less* but *better*—less clutter and more quality products, fewer random commitments and more fulfilling projects—I became less stressed *and* felt as though I was experiencing more success.

Have More Fun

A few months ago, I sat in my office working on a project. Lunchtime rolled around, and my phone buzzed on the table next to me. It was a text from a friend I hadn't seen in months. "Hey, I know this is random, but I'm on your side of town. Any chance you could meet for a spontaneous lunch in about twenty minutes?"

Normally I'd say I couldn't make it and ask whether we could schedule something for another day.

Just as I was about to text her back and say I couldn't swing it, I was reminded that life is short and I need to find ways to enjoy it.

I texted, "Sure! I can meet you then!" It felt like the most rebellious thing I'd done in a long time.

Dang, I thought as I pulled out of my driveway. *You've really gotta live a little more, J.*

After the waitress showed us to our table, we sat down and both subconsciously let out a sigh of relief in the middle of a busy day. We laughed and began to cram as much conversation as we could into the single hour we had.

Toward the end of our lunch, I took one of the last bites of my salad and said, "Gosh, I'm so glad we did this."

She sipped her lemonade. "Girl, me too! We started small businesses so we could have flexibility, and we need to allow ourselves to enjoy the benefits of the type of work we do."

She was so right.

Regardless of what your occupation is, there's a lesson to be learned here: A life of more possibility, more whimsy, and more contentment doesn't always require a full-blown makeover. Neither does it require that you check off every goal within the time frame you set when you were twelve and thought the world was a mystical land where every dream comes true simply because you wished upon a star. Oftentimes it requires only making a few adjustments right where you are so that you can find ways to enjoy the life you already have on the journey to where you're going.

For me, it took letting go of my first business, pivoting my professional plans in the face of a pandemic, losing two precious babies, launching a project that basically flopped, redefining what enough looks like for me, releasing my expectations, and letting go of the vision I had for my home to rediscover the importance of this. At first, delayed, disrupted, or destroyed plans seem to nullify our dreams altogether. However, now I can see that experiences like these can actually help us live more fulfilled lives *along the way,* not only when we get to a desired destination.

Perhaps the most important part of boot camp seasons like this is learning the art of being present and having fun right where we are—choosing to be spontaneous, laughing till we cry in the middle of a workday, learning something new, or finding a hobby even if we're not very good at it (ahem, gardening). Doing this helps us eliminate the tendency to live by a to-do list and overcome the pressure to live up to unrealistic expectations.

We all need a little more whimsy and delight—and both devastating moments and disappointments can invite us to prioritize these things more. Don't forget to give yourself permission to have a little more fun, no matter how old you are.

Welcome to Boot Camp

Focusing on the small things, creating rhythms and routines, learning something new, serving others, simplifying my life, and making more space for fun and spontaneity are just a few things I've done during my boot camp. I hope they provide you with some helpful ideas of where you might be able to start. Whatever your boot camp looks like, take this time to evaluate how well you've really stewarded your body, mind, soul, relationships, and time. Then consider what steps you can take to tend to them even just a little bit better.

Here's the thing: when dreams don't work out, you can

view your current situation as a dead end *or* as a training ground to help you fulfill your God-given destiny.

This entire life—not just the seasons of waiting—is a boot camp. It's preparation for our eternal home. All the more reason to tend to it well at all times, not just when things are hard.

Maybe a secret to success as we navigate heartbreak, waiting, or disappointment on the road toward our greatest dreams isn't simply being strong. I think, in fact, it's learning how to steward well—to plant in faith, tend with patience, and remain rooted in Love.

When we allow disrupted, delayed, and even seemingly destroyed dreams to invite us into more of what matters, everything will shift. And we'll always find so much power in releasing control of what is finite and temporary, sowing seeds into eternity, and saying yes to what matters most (and no to what doesn't).

Allow this to be a time when you discover what you want to grow and what you want to let go. Lean into the Lord. Connect with others. Admit what you don't know. Learn new things. And dang it—make room for margin and have a little more fun too.

Remember, this is your temporary home. Even when you get something you long for on this side of heaven, that milestone was never designed to be your final destination. And it will satisfy only for so long. There will almost always be something new to wait on or work toward. Dare to push back against the temptation to allow a waiting season to become a wasted season, or you'll miss out on your whole life. Because all of life is pretty much one big waiting room anyway. So, maybe here, in the middle, the challenge is to make the most of it.

Fill your life with the fun, the whimsy, the faith, and the love it needs so that you can get up again and put yourself back in the ring, just like the good steward and warrior you were created to be.

13

Finish Strong

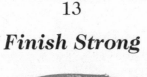

I'm writing this to you from Montana. We made it here, although this time by an airplane. It's been a while since our first attempt—you know, the one that ended somewhere in Minnesota with thousands of dollars lost on the Airbnb we had to forgo.

I'm looking out the window at the mountain range painted against the big sky. Nothing about this place is at all what I imagined it would be. It's better.

As I've stood in the vastness of its open plains surrounded by mountainous terrain and skies that stretch as far as the eye can see, I've had a deep appreciation for its beauty. I'm really savoring each dining or hiking experience, breathing in the mountain air, and taking time to be present and soak up every second. The big skies, friendly folks, and huge mountains we've been climbing are giving me a glimpse of what is possible and daring me to dream again just when dreaming seemed impossible.

I'm not sure I would have been so intentional, noticed every detail, or felt the gratitude for the respite and restoration this place is providing had my route here not been a bit nonlinear.

On the other hand, it's strange to think that I've made it to Montana but haven't arrived at the life that Montana has come to represent for me—the one where everything in my life feels in place and complete.

Have you ever experienced that strange feeling, the sense that things aren't quite how they were supposed to be (at least not how you thought they were supposed to be) even if where you are is full of loveliness?

It's weird yet sanctifying, isn't it? The reminder of what's missing against the backdrop of what you don't want to miss can create an unusual intersection of grief and gratitude. It's in these moments that I think we can really lean into liking our lives. We may not be head over heels in love with every aspect. There may still be some things out of place. But perhaps it is possible to deeply feel the tension of what hasn't gone right while appreciating the gift and beauty right here, in the middle.

We might not reach the destination that we're dreaming of easily or quickly, and we might even lose some resources in the pursuit. We might have to wait awhile or change our plans. But if we hold our vision in mind, keep a clear priority one day at a time, and plant seeds of legacy on each long and hard day, then when we get to where we're ultimately going—eternity—it will be worth every rejection, disappointment, long wait, and detour along the way.

A friend recently said to me, "When you experience loss

or setbacks *before* you get to your destination, it makes the magic of arriving so much sweeter."

If I experienced that on a small scale with my expectations and hopes about Montana being blown out of the water after U-turns and delayed gratification, then perhaps I can choose to believe that will be true of the destination Montana represents for me: Wholeness. Redemption of our stories. Restored dreams.

As hard as it may be to believe in the midst of shattered plans and disrupted dreams, maybe we can commit to believing it together when our plans don't go according to plan or when setbacks or suffering seem to disrupt the journey to where we hope to go.

Before Happily-Ever-After Happens

You know, this isn't how this book was supposed to end. I had an entirely different final chapter drafted one year ago. Everything was tied up with a pretty little bow, just how I like it.

The first time I turned in this manuscript, it was just ten days before I found out about our second loss. I had told this beautiful full-circle story and written all sorts of inspiring lessons about how if you just hold on and believe, you'll get your happy ending.

Although I think we all lean toward doing this, as an author I've come to find I like to pencil in my own happy ending before I actually get there.

When I sent it to my editor the first time, I included a

note about the last chapter, which was only about 90 percent complete, and told her I would finalize the details of the end in a few more weeks. I just wanted to be extra sure things would work out before finishing the beautiful redemption story that was *supposed* to be.

Of course, as you know, that's not how it went at all. My plans for this book blew up just like my plans for that year, just when I thought it was only a few paragraphs away from being complete. It was *almost* done, and I've since had to rewrite it entirely.

Is there anything as discouraging as being just inches away from a happy ending, only to have the entire thing blow up and be forced to start over? Not just in a book but in your real life story? I vote no—no, there is not. It's the most maddening thing.

I guess the fact that I didn't feel it was completely finished is significant. I *wanted* to tell the perfect happy ending that I'd written in my mind. I thought I was writing it to you on the other side of broken dreams, and I wanted to offer you proof of the cliché advice that if it doesn't work out on the first try, it will if you just get up and try again.

Of course, life doesn't always work out that way. Sometimes, as soon as you've gotten up from the last blow, you get knocked down again and might even begin to question your dreams entirely.

So, I've had to rewrite the story how it actually went, and that hasn't been an easy task . . . because this isn't the story I *wanted* to write—let alone live. This might have been the hardest project I've worked on to date, and if I'm honest, it frustrates the heck out of me that it's not tied up in a bow and that there are still a lot of unknowns. I thought I'd be writing to you from the other side. But instead, I've written to you from the middle. I guess, though, that's strangely appropriate.

Although I'd love for this to have been an easier experience, I've dared to wonder something: Is it possible that this is a better story and that I am becoming better because of it?

Here's what I mean: Nestled inside the heartbreaks and disappointments on the way to my dreams, I've uncovered those unexpected gains I told you about.

In the in-between, almost-but-not-quite, and unknown, I've experienced a *refining*. I've been transformed from the inside out, gained a new perspective on what truly matters, learned how to set healthy boundaries (even when it comes to working on my dreams), and discovered the power of knowing what you really want in a world that tells you that you should want it all.

I don't want to do *everything*. I want to do a few things—and do them well.

I don't want to flip houses I hardly have time to renovate, just because that looks fun on HGTV. I want to focus on my health and my family.

I don't want a Pinterest-perfect house. I want a functional home that is right for *me*—that I enjoy living in and that serves me, my family, and my community well.

I don't want to chase arbitrary financial goals just because someone else is making a certain amount. I want to run *my* race and make the money I need to fund my mission and create options for my family.

I don't want to be a harsh, demanding, or competitive

"girl boss." I simply want to think like a boss and set healthy boundaries so I don't burn out.

I don't want to keep up with, outdo, or work like men, just to achieve something. I want to lean into, embrace, and work in ways that support my feminine needs.

I don't want to do stuff just to prove to everyone else that I'm successful. I want to be a good steward who is intentional.

I could go on, but I'm sure you get the point. In the most unexpected way, the most unwanted setbacks and suffering reset my vision, reminded me of what I truly want, and clarified my aim—my mission. Now I know what I'm after . . . and what I absolutely am *not* after.

I want this clarity for you too.

Maybe you haven't arrived at your happily-ever-after yet. I bet there's something that still feels outstanding in your life. I don't mean *outstanding* in the sense of something great. I mean the still-to-be-done kind of *outstanding*. I call that a "pending dream." It's like staring at that annoying loading symbol on your computer when it freezes in the middle of an important project. You sit there, wondering how long it's going to take to just work already.

Can I let you in on a little secret? I don't think we ever really reach happily-ever-after on this side of heaven. We might reach a milestone, we might achieve a goal, but to think we'll get to a place where we finally have it all in a broken world? We're only fooling ourselves.

Part of me still wanted to wait to finish this book until I had that redemption story to tell. I wanted to tell a story with a picture-perfect ending.

I think we tend to pencil in our preferred redemption stories, how we want our stories to end after rough chapters. And then sometimes we end up facing another rough chapter and another, and we wake up to the reality that we aren't the authors of our own stories. I still wholeheartedly believe it'll ultimately end beautifully, but the story or the hard chapters may go on longer than we'd like—and truthfully, that's annoying.

I suppose this is the part where we must remember that they aren't our redemption stories to write. They're His. We aren't better authors than God is, and as much as we'd like Him to get on with it and pencil in the plot twist where we win, we must remember that, well, He already did. Two thousand years ago, on a cross. And this present circumstance isn't a dead end. In the middle of the mess, it's frustrating, maddening, and exhausting, but we can dig deep and find a way to believe that someday this crap will all make sense. Because there is more to my story and more to yours too.

The truth is, even if we get to a desired destination or reach a milestone, we're always in the middle—between two gardens, *almost* but not yet where we really long to be.

Finish *Well*

If you read the introduction of this book, you know the story of when I ran track in high school and, in my very first race, decided to lean over the finish line in an attempt to finish first but instead promptly face-planted on the track. I almost won . . . but then finished last.

I was so focused on beating someone else that I missed

my step and didn't finish well. Now, as I pursue hopes, dreams, and goals, I must ask myself, *Am I setting myself up to face-plant, or am I setting myself up to finish strong? Am I just trying to outdo or keep up with someone else? Or am I running at a sustainable pace, with my focus on what matters most, so I can finish my race well?*

You know, once you've been so close to reaching a goal or fulfilling a dream only to face-plant, it can be hard to find the courage to get up and try again. To start again. To run again. To put yourself out there again. To dream again.

Whether it's trying to get a promotion, find love, repair a relationship, or build a family, it's scary, vulnerable, and humbling to give your almosts another shot.

But listen—you don't have to finish first. You don't even have to finish fast. You don't have to finish in a flashy way or ahead of someone else. You don't even have to finish everything. Some things are better left on pause or undone if they're not the right things for you to focus on. But in the middle, as you await whatever it is that may feel out of reach, make it your mission to just finish *something*.

It feels good to finish something, even if it's not your greatest dream. Set a small goal, start on it, and don't quit until you finish. Whether that goal is to plant a garden, open a small business, or run a 5k, find something you can finish even if you're waiting on a dream.

Who Will You Become?

I have one last story for you. Not long ago, I shared a long conversation over breakfast with a business colleague turned dear friend. As we swapped stories of our disappointments and defeats on the road to our greatest dreams, the conversation came back to one core theme: when the road gets long or when things almost but then don't quite work out, it can make us *bitter* or it can make us *better*.

Then she said, "You know, there have been so many times in my life when what I wanted didn't exactly happen how I thought it should. Sometimes it has felt like I've had more disappointments than dreams come true. But now I can see how every struggle and setback along the way made me the woman I am today."

Every struggle and setback along the way made me the woman I am today.

As much as we'd like to write the perfect happy ending to our very unpredictable stories, sometimes it's not as simple as just getting up and trying again. Sometimes it takes asking for help, looking for gains in the pain, and inching our way forward—even if we must crawl first.

The challenges we'll encounter on the road to our greatest dreams are as unpredictable as the weather in Indiana. I'm beginning to realize that achieving every dream isn't all that matters. It also matters who we become and what we do, *even* when our dreams let us down.

Does that mean we should give up on our hopes? Absolutely not. But they may be refined through the fire, and in the fire, we may discover that some of the goals we were pursuing aren't actually a priority to us. Hardship and unmet expectations really have a way of shifting our focus from the unimportant and urgent to the most important and eternal—if we let them.

So, that's where I'm starting again. I'm persisting. I'll keep tending to things that matter instead of hustling to keep up or win a game I was never born to play. I'll keep planting in faith and rooting myself in Love. I'll keep taking one step forward at a time.

I hope that somehow, regardless of how many disappointments or heartbreaks you've faced, you'll dig deep and find just enough grit and grace to do the same.

I want to close with this: The back-to-back losses I experienced showed me just how many things had to come together perfectly for you and me to even have been born and draw breath on this earth. If one little cell splits wrong, that can be the end of someone's existence.

Do you know what that means? It means your life is no casual, simple thing. I just want you to understand how miraculous your very existence is. I hope that you cherish it. I hope that you go after life with reckless abandon. I hope that you don't give up and that you dare to be so dang persistent it hurts.

And in the meantime, in the tension between where you are and where you hope to be, continue to water the soil of your dreams and hold on to the hope that at the right time they will sprout, grow, and flourish . . . even if that process or timeline looks entirely different than you'd think.

If your dreams have been delayed, painfully disrupted, or even royally destroyed, how will you lean into that refining?

If you're dealing with unmet expectations, unachieved goals, or paralyzing unknowns, make it your mission to finish *something*, to keep going, and to remain faithful in the divine middle ground, even before you get to where you want to be. Run *your* race well.

Let's choose to live with intention during the almosts and in-betweens so that one day, at the end of our lives, we can look back and confidently say, "That was really hard. But 'I have fought the good fight, I have finished the race, I have kept the faith.'[1] And dang it—I'm thankful it made me the woman I am today."

Acknowledgments

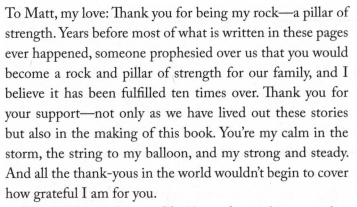

To Matt, my love: Thank you for being my rock—a pillar of strength. Years before most of what is written in these pages ever happened, someone prophesied over us that you would become a rock and pillar of strength for our family, and I believe it has been fulfilled ten times over. Thank you for your support—not only as we have lived out these stories but also in the making of this book. You're my calm in the storm, the string to my balloon, and my strong and steady. And all the thank-yous in the world wouldn't begin to cover how grateful I am for you.

To my babies in heaven: Thank you for teaching me what a mother's love is like and, as a result, allowing me to see the depth of the Father's love for His children. I will treasure your short but precious lives until the day I die. Although I wish you were here with me, you helped me see what really matters most in this life in a way I'm not sure much else could have. Outside of your existence, that is perhaps one of the greatest gifts you could have given me.

To my parents: Thank you for the ways you've dropped everything to be by my side during both the happiest and the darkest days of my life. Your unending support is a gift I don't take lightly. So many of the lessons in these pages are all thanks to you. If only the world could know how truly amazing you both are.

To my brother: Thank you for being the kind of brother every girl wishes she had and for always showing up at just the right time with the encouragement, strength, and faith I need to lean on. I'm so thankful for how you've grown, who you've become, and how you speak life into me when I need it most. I couldn't have gotten through this season of my life or found the strength to write half of these words without you.

To my publishing team at Penguin Random House and WaterBrook: Thank you for the hard work and dedication you've shown this project. I am immensely grateful for your flexibility when dates had to change and for your commitment to making this the best it could be, even when I would have preferred to rush it through to completion. Your ongoing guidance, grace, and support have made me a better writer and leader, and I am so thankful.

To those in my Jordan Lee Media team, both past and present: Thank you for all the hard work you've put in to make this (and all the other projects I tackle) a success. You are a gift.

To my online community, podcast listeners, and readers: Thank you for supporting my work through the years. Thank you for honoring my story. Thank you for reading these pages and sharing these words with your friends. I couldn't do any of this without you.

Finally, all glory to God for writing stories that rarely make much sense in the middle but always have more meaning and beauty hidden inside than we could ever ask or imagine.

Notes

Chapter 1:
Redefine Success

1. Lexico, s.v. "ambition," www.lexico.com/en/
   definition/ambition.

Chapter 2:
Letting Go of a Good Thing

1. Bob Goff, "You Have Permission to Dream Big,"
   interview by Jordan Lee Dooley, *She* (podcast),
   July 1, 2020, https://jordanleedooley.com/
   you-have-permission-to-dream-big.

Chapter 7:
Unexpected Gains from Unwanted Pain

1. Lexico, s.v. "refine," www.lexico.com/en/
   definition/refine.
2. Exodus 23:10–11.

Chapter 9:
When Your Dreams Come True for
Everyone Else but You

1. Romans 12:15.

Chapter 10:
Uproot the Lies You Believe

1. Jerry Sittser, *A Grace Disguised: How the Soul Grows Through Loss,* rev. ed. (Grand Rapids, MI: Zondervan, 2004), 122–24.
2. Ephesians 3:17–19.

Chapter 11:
Prioritize Your Priority

1. Greg McKeown, *Essentialism: The Disciplined Pursuit of Less* (New York: Crown Business, 2014), 16.
2. McKeown, *Essentialism,* 16.

Chapter 12:
Make the Most of the Almosts

1. Philippians 4:8.
2. Myquillyn Smith, *Cozy Minimalist Home: More Style, Less Stuff* (Grand Rapids, MI: Zondervan, 2018), 34.

Chapter 13:
Finish Strong

1. 2 Timothy 4:7.

About the Author

By equipping women to clarify what they truly value (and what they don't!), JORDAN LEE DOOLEY is on a mission to eliminate the lie that we must do it all and have it all to be successful. Fueled by a passion for helping women pursue their dreams while prioritizing their health and well-being, she has built a massive online community to guide ambitious women toward a more sustainable, intentional way of life. Her words and influence continue to expand daily as she serves up practical advice, expert insight, and inspiring stories on her top-rated podcast and social media channels. Jordan, an Indiana girl born and raised, is happily married to her college sweetheart and calls a small town outside of Indianapolis home.

About the Type

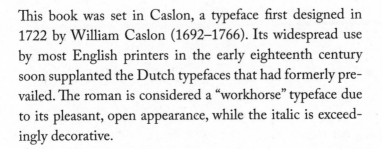

This book was set in Caslon, a typeface first designed in 1722 by William Caslon (1692–1766). Its widespread use by most English printers in the early eighteenth century soon supplanted the Dutch typefaces that had formerly prevailed. The roman is considered a "workhorse" typeface due to its pleasant, open appearance, while the italic is exceedingly decorative.

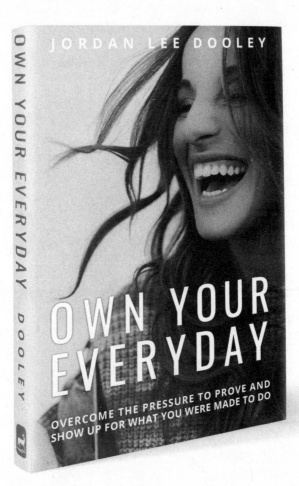